Wright's Writings:
Reflections on Culture
and Politics 1894–1959

T0327286

Wright's Writings:
Reflections on Culture
and Politics 1894–1959

Kenneth Frampton

Columbia Books on
Architecture and the City

Wright's Writings: Reflections on Culture and Politics 1894–1959 features extensive images from the Frank Lloyd Wright Foundation Archives (The Museum of Modern Art | Avery Architectural and Fine Arts Library, Columbia University, New York). The author and publisher express their gratitude to all three organizations for the use of these images, which have been newly photographed by Avery Architectural and Fine Arts Library. Full credit information can be found on the image credits page.

These introductory essays were written in 1992 on the occasion of Rizzoli's publishing of Frank Lloyd Wright's complete literary work between 1894–1959 in the five-volume book, *Frank Lloyd Wright: Collected Writings*, edited by Bruce Brooks Pfeiffer. They appear here with the gracious permission of the publisher and the Frank Lloyd Wright Foundation.

1939–1949   82

Surely the most surprising things about Wright's writing during this period are his pacifism and his opposition to US involvement in the war. At this time, Wright also thought that the US was ungovernable due to its size, and advocated dividing it into thee separate sovereign states. The essays during this decade also document the beginning of Wright's public debates with Robert Moses over the Guggenheim Museum.

1949–1959   112

Much of what Wright wrote in the last decade of his life reworked the themes he had already broached in the previous half-century. *The Natural House* of 1954 and *The Living City* of 1958 are both summations of his Usonian vision to which he added the celebratory *The Story of the Tower* of 1956.

Wright at Avery

Carole Ann Fabian

Director, Avery Architectural and Fine Arts Library

In 2012, Avery Architectural and Fine Arts Library together with the Museum of Modern Art coacquired the singularly expansive Frank Lloyd Wright Foundation Archives. Among the more than 32,000 Wright drawings, 300,000 sheets of correspondence, 285 films, 40,000 photographs, and records of the Taliesin Associated Architects are 2,784 manuscripts of Wright's published and unpublished works. The manuscripts document the evolution of Wright's thought in written form from first drafts to editor's proofs to final publication versions, and they reveal the intellectual journey that Wright traveled as he prepared lectures, essays, and books over the course of his career. From the manuscript for his first speech to his last written work, Wright's prolific bibliographic legacy is interwoven and examined in Avery's stacks and archives. The essays in this book help us reframe and discover new ways of reading Wright's extensive literary project alongside the political, material, and social worlds he navigated; and it is only with the growing accessibility of this archive that such a focused examination of Wright's ideas is possible.

Frank Lloyd Wright's architecture practice was established in 1893, nearly coincident with the founding of Avery Library in 1890. In 1894, Wright delivered his first public lecture, "The Architect and the Machine," at the Architectural League of America in Chicago and, in their first published form, Wright's words entered Avery Library's collection as "The Architect" in the September 1900 issue of *The Brickbuilder*. Now, more than one hundred years later, the manuscript for that lecture and thousands of other primary documents by Wright join Avery's comprehensive collection of Wright's bibliography. Avery's Wright holdings include over 1,200 books by and about Wright in the general collections and more than two hundred rare Wright editions, including *House Beautiful* (1896–1898), *Ausgeführte Bauten und Entwürfe* (1910 and subsequent editions), and *The Japanese Print* (1912). In addition, the Avery Classics collection holds fifty books from his son John Lloyd Wright's library and 116 volumes of Wright's own copies of his published works, many annotated and inscribed, including *An Autobiography* (1943) and his last written work, the preamble to the proposed book *The Wonderful World of Architecture*, published posthumously in *Architecture: Man in Possession of His Earth* (1962).

Similarly, the Avery Index to Architectural Periodicals traces articles authored by and about Wright; the preponderance of interest in Wright is notable with more than 3,100 entries in twenty languages. In comparison to articles by and about his peers — early contemporaries such as McKim, Mead & White, his fellow modernist Le Corbusier, and form-shaping architects of our times such as Frank Gehry—more journal articles are written and indexed about Wright than any other architect.

The Wright bibliography—monographic and serial publications—is consulted side-by-side with the architectural records held in the Avery Drawings and Archives collections. Creative and critical lines of thought stretch across Avery's archival holdings, connecting Wright to the papers of closely associated architects, historians, and critics including Henry-Russell Hitchcock, Douglas Putnam Haskell, Louis Sullivan, Edgar J. Kaufmann, Philip Johnson, and Edgar Tafel, each offering comment on Wright or including drawings and documents authored or drawn by Wright himself. From Avery's Frank Lloyd Wright Collection of Louis Henry Sullivan Drawings to drawings by Sullivan discovered in the Frank Lloyd Wright Foundation Archives, there is a poetic reciprocity and metaphorical conversation across the archives about Wright, architecture, and its critique.

Since the archive's acquisition, research interest in Wright has reawakened. Wright experts and researchers are examining the iconic figure from new perspectives with the benefit of unprecedented access to the Wright archive at Avery; and from their studies, new scholarship is emerging. Newly published works including Neil Levine's *The Urbanism of Frank Lloyd Wright* (2015); Paul Turner's *Frank Lloyd Wright and San Francisco* (2016); and Kenneth Frampton's *Writings on Wright* (2017), a compiled edition of his introductory essays to Bruce Brooks Pfeiffer's five volume *Frank Lloyd Wright: Collected Writings* (1992) re-invigorate our examination of Wright. *Frank Lloyd Wright at 150: Unpacking the Archive* (2017), a major exhibition and accompanying catalogue, celebrates Wright's anniversary year and is copresented by Avery and MoMA as an outgrowth of their shared stewardship of the archive. This project in particular demonstrates an intensive interrogation of the archive through diverse lines of inquiry by fifteen scholars who, together with Barry Bergdoll, cocurated the exhibition and authored essays that open Wright's work to new interpretations and new audiences. These publications add to Avery's enduring commitment to collect the Wright bibliography, now greatly amplified by the acquisition of Wright's monumental archive, and continue to provoke an exploration of the meaning of "architecture—the mother of art of human-kind" (Frank Lloyd Wright, 1959).

Approaching Wright

Barry Bergdoll

Meyer Schapiro Professor of Art History and Archaeology,
Columbia University

Frank Lloyd Wright has been a sustained object of Kenneth Frampton's reflections on the larger cultural and ideological stakes of modern architecture for over a quarter of a century. The protean American architect has been as central to his writings, since the first edition of *Modern Architecture: A Critical History* in 1980, as to his teaching in lectures, seminars, and analytical model-making at Columbia University. Needless to say, Frampton was among those who most enthusiastically joined the welcoming committee when it was announced in 2012 that the thousands of documents—drawings, letters, manuscripts, photographs, films, ephemera, and many of Wright's own books—that form the Frank Lloyd Wright Foundation Archives were to be transferred to the Avery Architectural and Fine Arts Library, as part of an innovative co-stewardship arrangement with the Museum of Modern Art. Coincidentally it was also the fortieth anniversary of Frampton's own arrival to Morningside Heights. To pair one of the most influential architectural critic/historians of modernity with one of the towering figures of modern architecture was one of the myriad ways in which the acquisition of Wright's drawings and papers has enriched both the Avery Library and the University.

From the very outset of the first of the two chapters devoted to Wright in *Modern Architecture*, Frampton has seen him as an author as much as an architect, giving pride of place to Wright's writings in what he defines as Wright's lifelong vocation of "the transformation of industrial technique through art." And from the first, Frampton has engaged in a complex "interweaving"—a Framptonian and Wrightian theme via Gottfried Semper—of Wright's cultural and ideological creation of larger narratives of the origins and destiny of modern American culture in text with Wright's powerful creation of new spatial and tectonic expressions in building. With his 1991 book *Frank Lloyd Wright: A Primer in Architectural Principles,* Frampton carried that method through Wright's long career. There he traced themes at once in building and writing as Wright the architect moved across materials and structural experiments, negotiating continually between the crafting of the space of the family and a concern for the role of the larger community, be it defined in secular or sacred, commercial or political terms. Wright was at once an observer and an actor in a landscape being rewritten by the forces of technology from the automobile to the television, and Frampton revealed the extent to which the widely ranging scales of architectural thought, from the domestic interior to the continental settlement of the land, were in Wright's purview from his earliest work. In writing, Wright took up ambitious themes of architecture's relationship to nature, to democratic polity, to landscape, and, of course, to technology, all grappled with in prose as engaging, yet as riddled with seeming paradoxes and contradictions, as another key figure as important to Frampton as to Wright, namely, John Ruskin.

It was therefore an inspired choice when Frampton was invited to write a preface to each of the five volumes of Wright's collected writings edited by Bruce Brooks Pfeiffer and published by Rizzoli in the mid-1990s. These five prefatory essays — a format he has mastered over the years for both historical and contemporary figures — are collected together here in a single volume. To read them seamlessly is to discover for ourselves how these fragments coalesce into one of the most concise yet simultaneously broad and incisive treatments of the evolution of Wright's ideas on the tight matrix of architecture, society, and politics. At the same time, they are as valuable as roadmaps to the evolving contours of Wright's ideological and artistic positions as they are to following Frampton's own project as a critical historian.

Beginning in the 1980s, Frampton's increased engagement with Wright was exemplary of his own interweaving of history and criticism in the face of the rapid rise of postmodernism in architectural practice. Rejecting the increasingly acritical nostalgia of stylistic postmodernism that more and more in the 1980s came to color the architectural scene, particularly in the United States, Frampton developed an historical project that explicitly engaged with what he acknowledged as a critical history tinged with Frankfurt School influence. The work of Theodor Adorno, whose writings were so influential in East Coast architectural thinking and debate in the 1980s and 1990s, made Frampton "acutely aware," as he acknowledged in the 1980 introduction to *Modern Architecture,* "of the dark side of the Enlightenment which, in the name of an unreasonable reason, has brought man to a situation where he begins to be as alienated from his own production as from the natural world." It is not surprising therefore that Wright figured so prominently in Frampton's readings of modern architecture since the mid-eighteenth century in both Frampton's seminal survey text and his 1995 *Studies in Tectonic Culture.* Nor is it surprising the amount of attention that Frampton put into understanding what was at stake in Wright's own vision with regard to the possible horizons of architectural practice, concerns that went hand in hand with his articulation of a position developed under the clarion call of "Towards a Critical Regionalism," a quasi-manifesto first sketched in 1983.

Despite the brevity of the five texts gathered here, they offer a veritable compendium of key themes for treating Wright's idiosyncratic genius in relationship not only to the stakes of modernism in architecture but

14

also to the larger challenges of democratic society, as relevant in Wright's trajectory from the gilded age of the late nineteenth century via the Depression to the Cold War, in full force when he left the scene after seven decades of practice with his death in 1959. As overwhelming as the bibliography of Wright is — some 1085 books in the online catalogue of Columbia University and about twice as many articles in the Avery Index to Architectural Periodicals — there are many threads in these prefaces that have yet to be fully explored. One major rationale for bringing the vast Wright archive into the Avery Library was to open Wright's work to new lines of inquiry and into contexts that the often largely monographic approach has not fostered to the fullest extent possible. In historical terms Frampton suggested, for example, a study of the evolution of Wright's ideas about alternatives to university-based design education in relationship to the most powerful models on the horizon when the Taliesin Fellowship was put into place around 1932 — namely the (then threatened) Bauhaus as well as Eliel Saarinen's Cranbrook Academy. Frampton told us at one point that Wright's thought "seems even now to be surprisingly fresh and insightful," something that might well be said equally of these prefaces penned twenty-five years ago. Here are to be found invitations to look more deeply at Wright's reflections on "the emancipatory myth of American democracy," on his fascination with Soviet Russia and the various forms that a "categorical attack on land and money speculation" might take, on his engagement with radial theories of social credit, of land management, of pacifism, and on the sanguine embrace of new technologies. Frampton's synthetic readings of Wright's often convoluted texts invite us equally to bring historical contextualization and reflections on untimely resonances into dialogue.

1894–1930

Four rather slight essays separate Wright's first tentative formulations in his 1894 address "The Architect and the Machine" [page 25] from the epoch-making "The Art and Craft of the Machine" [page 27], first presented at Jane Addams's Hull-House in Chicago in 1901. In this last, Wright acknowledged his despair at first reading Victor Hugo's prophecy that architecture would be superseded by the printed word—by the advent of the rotary press, which, along with the teeming industrialized mass of the city of Chicago, would constitute the very essence of the machine for Wright. He concluded by reversing the logic and by arguing that only an intelligent application of machine production would be able to redeem the excesses of mechanization, that is to say, would be able to imbue the mercantile nineteenth-century capital city with the essence of a soul.

In his 1897 essay "Architect, Architecture, and the Client" [page 26], Wright had already arrived at the prerequisites of a new domesticity, anticipating the labor-saving kitchen by some sixteen years prior to Christine Frederick publishing her *Ladies' Home Journal* articles as a book, *The New Housekeeping: Efficiency Studies in Home Management*, in 1913. In the same essay he opposed freestanding radiators or freestanding anything for that matter, except furniture. Indeed, Wright's new American home was largely couched at this time in negative terms, as a cleaning of the Augean stables. Thus, he came out against pictures for their capacity to destroy the repose of the interior and against direct artificial lighting for much the same reason. He repudiated the use of gilt in any form and advocated for the use of natural wood and plaster, stained so as to convey a sense of sempiternal warmth, in conjunction with dried fresh flowers artfully displayed in well-appointed vases.

The ideological ramifications of all this were elaborated at an abstract level in his address "The Philosophy of Fine Art" [page 28], delivered at the Art Institute of Chicago in 1917, where he compared the laws of form to musical harmonies and went on to insist that true art must be based on conventionalization. Elsewhere Wright railed against the fashionable "plan factory" architect and asserted, long before Le Corbusier, that architecture is largely a matter of organization, while its formal syntax must be derived from nature with a capital N. Given the primacy Wright attached to Nature at every conceivable juncture, seeing it as the embodiment of the godhead itself, it is altogether surprising that he said so little about the art of landscapes — save for expressing his passing admiration for the gardens of Gertrude Jekyll.

That he became an exceptionally experienced home builder during the first decade of the twentieth century was borne out by the thirty-three Prairie houses of widely varying size realized between 1900 and 1910 and by the various innovatory devices that he used in their construction: from the long-span steel beams of the Robie House to the cement and plaster partitions applied to both sides of metal lathing; from the application of reinforced concrete to domestic construction to the use of built-in vacuum systems and the application of side-hung casement windows in opposition to the classical American preference for the guillotine sash window.

The outward swinging casement is prominently featured in his first manifesto, "In the Cause of Architecture," published in *Architectural Record* in May 1908. In this six-point manifesto Wright argued for a domestic architecture characterized by simplicity, repose, economy, horizontal windows, discrete ornaments, built-in furniture, undressed natural materials, and the full integration of the building into its site. Having thus established his basic precepts, Wright formulated his concept of "constitutional ornament," that is to say, ornament that is integrated into, rather than applied to the fabric of a building: a preference for structural decoration rather than decorated structure, to cite the distinction coined by Auguste Perret. At the same time, after mounting a categorical attack on the barbarism of the Renaissance, he admitted to being profoundly influenced by the Japanese print.

18

These are the twin themes that he returned to in his next two essays: first, in the polemical pro-Gothic introduction with which he opened the 1910 Wasmuth volumes, *Ausgefürte Bauten und Entwürfe* [pages 29–31]; second, in his homage to Japanese civilization that first appeared with his initial essay on the Japanese woodblock print, *The Japanese Print* [page 32]. This latter essay afforded him a further occasion on which to elaborate his views as to the nature of the decorative:

> The ultimate value of a Japanese print will be measured by the extent to which it distills, or rather exhales, this precious quality called "decorative." We generally do not quite understand what that means and are apt to use the term slightingly—especially when compared with "art," which has supposedly some other and greater mission. I—speaking for myself—do not know what other mission it legitimately could have, but I am sure of this at least, that the rhythmic play of parts, the poise and balance, the respect the forms pay to the surface treated, and the repose these qualities attain to and impart and which together constitutes what we call good decoration, are really the very life of all true graphic art whatsoever. In the degree that the print possesses this quality, it is abidingly precious; this quality determines—and constitutes its intrinsic value.[1]

This was by no means Wright's last word on Japanese culture, for he wrote three further introductory essays between 1912 and 1927, and later still indulged in the annual fall "print party" ritual at the Taliesin Fellowship, in which he habitually displayed his print collection. For Wright, the Japanese print remained the ethical shibboleth with which he would always be able to attack the "pompier bourgeois" taste of the Renaissance. Moreover, much like the role played by the purist canvas in Le Corbusier's architecture, the print, for Wright, was an icon that embodied the essence of an entire civilization.

The received historical accounts of Wright's career to date have tended, for inexplicable reasons, to ignore two seminal creations of the later Prairie period. The first of these is the design for a prototypical subdivision submitted for the City Club of Chicago competition of 1913, the principles of which were summed up by Wright three years later in an essay in the competition publication, *City Residential Land Development*, edited by Alfred B. Yeomans and published in May 1916 [page 33]. The second remarkable achievement is the Imperial Hotel in Tokyo, under construction from 1916 to 1922, and its even more miraculous survival of the Kantō earthquake of 1923.

Wright's 1913 "city-in-miniature" is a hypothetical urban synthesis of all the prototypical Prairie forms that he had evolved between his Francisco Terrace Apartments (Chicago 1985) and his Midway Gardens (Chicago 1914), including such key projects as the Larkin Building (1904), Unity Temple (1906), City National Bank, Mason City (1909), the various Prairie houses of the period, the quadruple block plan (comprising four houses, each with different aspects and pinwheeling about a central core), and even his first sketches for Aline Barnsdall's Olive Hill Theater.

In principle, all of these types were somehow incorporated into Wright's prototypical "park-city" that was far more cogent and discretely scaled in its various dispositions than anything attained in the realized garden city prototypes of the period, such as Letchworth in England. Moreover, it was an imminently realizable vision of middle-class civility unfortunately never attained in America or elsewhere. Wright's subsequent deurbanization theory, beginning with *The Disappearing City* of 1932, veered toward a rather abstract vision dominated by mechanization. In retrospect this seems to have been the last moment when the form of a specific urbanity could still be imagined just prior to the apocalypse of motopia. It was Wright's Oak Park critique of Daniel Burnham's monumental "city beautiful" Chicago plan of 1909.

Wright's diminutive neighborhood unit was an apotheosis of American Progressivism, directly related to the Chicago School of urban sociology and educational reform, to the revisionist social consensus shared by such intellectuals as Jane Addams, John Dewey, Thorstein Veblen, and Charles Horton Cooley, whose book *Social Organization* was published in 1909. Wright's City Club plan was organized in such a way as to facilitate the maintenance of Cooley's primary social groups: the family, the kindergarten, and the neighborhood unit. Evidently indebted to Jens Jensen and the Chicago park system, Wright's park-city was designed to facilitate a pattern of social interaction that was capable of compensating for the loss of the small town. This mythic "city-in-miniature" was thus intended to serve as a socially integrative settlement pattern in which the workers' low-rise, high-density collective housing could be mixed with quadruple-block houses grouped in clusters of four — the whole being inextricably woven together like a carpet, particularly in respect to its socio-cultural, educational, and recreational facilities. The aim was to raise the level of the society through a process of spatial acculturation. It was perhaps the last reformist effort, as Roger Cranshaw has remarked, to transcend the hegemony of industrialized capitalism through bourgeois moral reform; and it is no surprise that the church in Wright's plan, significantly called a "temple," is strictly nondenominational.[2]

Apart from the obituaries written on the occasion of Louis Sullivan's death in 1924, Wright's incidental writings between 1922 and 1925 are almost exclusively devoted to the achievement of the Imperial Hotel, which was in so many ways a homecoming for Wright in that it was a Xanadu built by a Westerner profoundly influenced by Japanese culture. In his essay, "The New Imperial Hotel" of 1923 [page 34], Wright made it only too clear how different his "garden-hotel" type was from the standard American "office-hotel" and how, with its 1,000-seat theater and 300-seat cabaret, it was intended to function as much as a general cultural center as a luxury residence. In this and other essays dedicated to the hotel he constantly remarked on the unprecedented combination of occidental and oriental types and on the difficulty of achieving such a synthesis, particularly given the precise but idiosyncratic character of the typical Japanese craftsman and the rather awkward labor-intensive methods employed by the Japanese building industry. Elsewhere he railed against the Japanese weakness for the steel-framed Yankee skyscrapers, many of which were destroyed in the 1923 earthquake. He expressed frustration over their depressing penchant for Western-style, neo-Renaissance emporia. The achievement of the spectacularly anti-seismic Imperial Hotel gave further proof, as though any were needed, of Wright's consummate skill as a builder, his ever-present inventiveness in dealing with unprecedented conditions—such as his prompt abandonment of steel plumbing halfway through construction, after learning of its propensity to rust in the Tokyo climate, or his equally ingenious but scandalous use of cheap Ōya lava stone for fair-faced revetment. In this regard he attributed the Japanese term *shibui* to his hotel, indicative of a quality that, while at first resisted by society, comes to be increasingly valued.

As far as his compulsive writing was concerned, Wright was never more revealing nor at the same time more diffuse and repetitive as he was in the numerous articles that he wrote for the editor of *Architectural Record*, M. A. Mikkelsen—the essays appearing more or less consecutively in 1927 and 1928, once again under the omnibus title "In the Cause of Architecture" [page 35]. While Wright was unduly rhetorical by nature, the main cause of the repetition on this occasion arose from the fact that the first year was a dry run to be followed by a final version, comprising nine installments published in 1928.

The main themes of these articles were by now somewhat predictable, such as the imperative to master the machine and the need to ground tectonic form in natural law. The term "Usonia," meaning the USA, first coined by Wright in 1925, reappears here with increasing frequency in light of Wright's advocacy of standardized modular construction, this being seen as a future guarantor of Usonian democracy. Wright likened this approach to weaving and to the warp and woof of an oriental rug, a metaphor also employed by Sullivan in accounting for the brick-faced construction of his Midwestern banks. Wright followed this by stressing the varying constitutive and expressive capacities of different materials, and at this juncture he began to introduce, if not a new theme, a new discourse on the potential of relatively unprecedented materials and processes: wood veneer, plate-glass electroglazing, steel, sheet metal, and various kinds of modern joining and finishing techniques. Wright went out of his way to characterize both terracotta and concrete as "conglomera"—that is, nontectonic material.

In the first of the essays for the 1928 series, entitled "The Logic of the Plan" [page 35], Wright argued that the architect must prove his ability at the level of the ground plan or not at all (shades here of Le Corbusier's "the plan is the generator" of 1923). He went on to contend that the basic tectonic principle of his work as a whole was immediately readable from the plan. Thus, just as Unity Temple was an in situ concrete building, the Avery Coonley residence was destined to be framed in wood, and the Larkin Building had a plan that could only be realized through the use of brick.[3]

In later essays in this series, numbers VI, VII, and VIII, Wright began to formulate the component parts of his emerging Usonian aesthetic. He passed from the crystalline potential of glass to his first theoretical justification of the textile block system, and finally to the penultimate and most important essay of the series, devoted to sheet metal, wherein we encounter what is surely his most vivid description of a work—his 1924 proposal for the National Life Insurance offices in Chicago:

The exterior walls, as such, disappear—instead are suspended, standardized sheet-copper screens. The walls themselves cease to exist as either weight or thickness. Windows become in this fabrication a matter of a unit in the screen fabric, opening singly or in groups at the will of the occupant. All windows may be cleaned from the inside with neither bother nor risk. The vertical mullions (copper shells filled with non-conducting material) are large and strong enough only to carry from floor to floor and project much or little as shadow on the glass may or may not be wanted. More projection enriches the shadow. Less projection dispels the shadows and brightens the interior. These protecting blades of copper act in the sun like the blades of a blind.

The unit of two feet both ways is, in this instance, emphasized on every alternate vertical with additional emphasis on every fifth. There is no emphasis on the horizontal units. The edge of the various floors being beveled to the same section as is used between the windows, it appears in the screen as such horizontal division occurring naturally on the two-foot unit lines.

Being likewise fabricated on a perfect unit system, the interior partitions may all be made up in sections, complete with doors, ready to set in place and designing to match the general style of the outer wall screen.

These interior partition-units thus fabricated may be stored ready to use, and any changes to suit tenants may be made overnight with no waste of time and material.

The increase of glass area over the usual skyscraper fenestration is only about ten percent (the margin could be increased or diminished by expanding or contacting the copper members in which it is set), so the expense of heating is not materially increased. Inasmuch as the copper mullions are filled with insulating material and the window openings are tight, being mechanical units in a mechanical screen, this excess of glass is compensated.

The radiators are cast as a railing set in front of the glass unit of this outer screen wall, free enough to make cleaning easy.[4]

It is interesting to note that Wright conceived of the proposal's internal treelike cantilevered structure in different forms: in the first instance as a composite cantilever and in the second as a twin-stem structure with symmetrically cantilevered floors, linked by a bridge-span between the points of contraflexure. The essential continuity and articulation of Wright's magnum opus—his masterly SC Johnson Wax Administration Building of 1936—is already anticipated here in a dramatic synthesis of structural and membraceous form.

Repudiating the categories of style and composition and asserting in their place character and organic rhythm, Wright ended the 1920s defining beauty as a natural order "whether of the mind or the body, because we are Nature ourselves in this sense." He added to this the corollary that the curious is merely a disorder in nature. With this aphorism, Wright distanced himself from the European avant-garde and asserted his own cause, conservative in the deepest sense. Wright entered the 1930s unemployed and embittered, and his essays dating from early 1930 are little more than diatribes against all and sundry, against the profession, the AIA, and Henry-Russell Hitchcock, who just over a decade later produced his classic study of Wright's work, *In the Nature of Materials*.

Notes

1. Frank Lloyd Wright, *The Japanese Print: An Interpretation* (Chicago: Ralph Fletcher Seymour, Co., 1912), 20–21.
2. Roger Crenshaw, "Frank Lloyd Wright's Progressive Utopia," *Architectural Association Quarterly*, vol. 10, no. 1 (1978): 3–9.
3. In fact, the Larkin Building was a steel-framed brick clad construction.
4. Frank Lloyd Wright, "In the Cause of Architecture, VIII: Sheet Metal and a Modern Instance," *Architectural Record*, vol. 64, no. 4 (October 1928): 334–342.

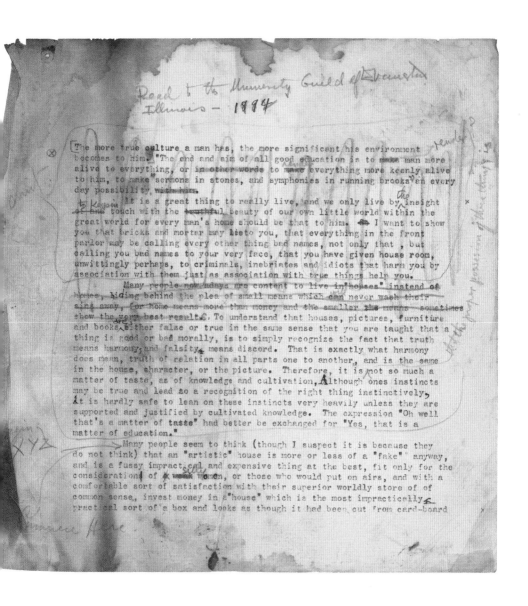

Road to the University Guild of Evanston
Illinois — 1894

The more true culture a man has, the more significant his environment becomes to him. "The end and aim of all good education is to make man more alive to everything, or in other words to make everything more keenly alive to him, to make "sermons in stones, and symphonies in running brooks" an every day possibility, with him.

It is a great thing to really live, and we only live by the insight and touch with the truthful beauty of our own little world within the great world for every man's home should be that to him. I want to show you that bricks and morter may beto you, that everything in the front parlor may be calling every other thing bad names, not only that, but calling you bad names to your very face, that you have given house room, unwittingly perhaps, to criminals, inebriates and idiots that harm you by association with them just as association with true things help you.

Many people nowadays are content to live in "houses" instead of homes, hiding behind the plea of small means which can never wash their sins away, for home means more than money and the smaller the means — sometimes show the very best result. To understand that houses, pictures, furniture and books, either false or true in the same sense that you are taught that a thing is good or bad morally, is to simply recognize the fact that truth means harmony and falsity means discord. That is exactly what harmony does mean, truth of relation in all parts one to another, and is the same in the house, character, or the picture. Therefore, it is not so much a matter of taste, as of knowledge and cultivation, Although ones instincts may be true and lead to a recognition of the right thing instinctively, it is hardly safe to lean on these instincts very heavily unless they are supported and justified by cultivated knowledge. The expression "Oh well that's a matter of taste" had better be exchanged for "Yes, that is a matter of education."

Many people seem to think (though I suspect it is because they do not think) that an "artistic" house is more or less of a "fake" anyway, and is a fussy impractical and expensive thing at the best, fit only for the consideration of weak women, or those who would put on airs, and with a comfortable sort of satisfaction with their superior worldly store of of common sense, invest money in a "house" which is the most impractically practical sort of a box and looks as though it had been cut from card-board

"The Architect and the Machine," read at the University Guild of Evanston, Illinois, 1894.

25

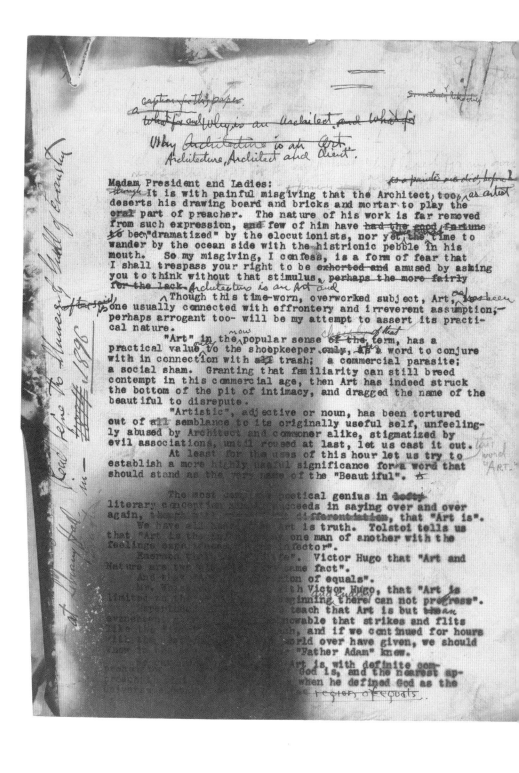

What for and Why is an Architect and what for

Why Architecture is an Art.
Architecture, Architect and Client.

Madam President and Ladies:

for a painter or did, before he

~~though~~ It is with painful misgiving that the Architect, too, *as artist*
deserts his drawing board and bricks and mortar to play the
~~oral~~ part of preacher. The nature of his work is far removed
from such expression, ~~and~~ few of him have ~~had the good fortune
to~~ been "dramatized" by the elocutionists, nor yet the time to
wander by the ocean side with the histrionic pebble in his
mouth. So my misgiving, I confess, is a form of fear that
I shall trespass your right to be ~~exhorted and~~ amused by asking
you to think without that stimulus, ~~perhaps the more fairly
for the lack.~~ *Architecture is an Art and*

          Though this time-worn, overworked subject, Art, *as has been*
~~so oft said~~ one usually connected with effrontery and irreverent assumption;—
perhaps arrogant too- will be my attempt to assert its practi-
cal nature.

      "Art" in the *now* popular sense ~~of the~~ *christening of that* term, has a
practical value *to* the shopkeeper ~~only, as a~~ word to conjure
with in connection with ~~all~~ trash; a commercial parasite;
a social sham. Granting that familiarity can still breed
contempt in this commercial age, then Art has indeed struck
the bottom of the pit of intimacy, and dragged the name of the
beautiful to disrepute.

      "Artistic", adjective or noun, has been tortured
out of all semblance to its originally useful self, unfeeling-
ly abused by Architect and commoner alike, stigmatized by
evil associations, until roused at last, let us cast it out.

      At least for the uses of this hour let us try to
establish a more highly useful significance for a word that
should stand as the very name of the "Beautiful". *this word "Art."*

      The most ~~original~~ poetical genius in ~~modern~~
literary conception ~~that~~ succeeds in saying over and over
again, ~~though with little actual differentiation,~~ that "Art is".

      We have ~~all heard that~~ Art is truth. Tolstoi tells us
that "Art is the ~~influence by~~ one man of another with the
feelings experienced ~~by the infector~~".

      Emerson that ~~Art is life~~". Victor Hugo that "Art and
Nature are two ~~...~~ same fact".

      And that ~~...~~ tion of equals".

      Mr. ~~...~~ th Victor Hugo, that "Art is
limited ~~...~~ ginning there can not progress".

      ~~...~~ teach that Art is but ~~the un~~
~~...~~ movable that strikes and flits
like the ~~...~~ h, and if we continued for hours
~~...~~ world over have given, we should
~~...~~ "Father Adam" knew.

      ~~...~~ Art is, with definite com-
~~...~~ God is, and the nearest ap-
~~...~~ when he defined God as the
region of equals.

"Architecture, Architect and Client," read at the University Guild of Evanston,
Illinois, 1896.

Note read at Hull.
House Chicago -
1901 -Feb.
later read at Milwaukee
Cincinati — + Chicago Art Institute by F.LL.W)

THE ART AND CRAFT OF THE MACHINE
BY FRANK LLOYD WRIGHT

No one, I hope has come here to-night for a Sociological prescrip-
tion for the cure of evils peculiar to this Machine Age: - For I have come to

you as an Architect; to say my word for the right use of our mere tools. There

is no thrift in a craft until the tools are mastered; - There will be none in

Society until the elements by which it works are mastered; - There will be no

Art worth the man until these elements are grasped and idealized, truthfully by

Although these elements are common place, we as a people do not seem to understand

them - Although we probably have richer raw materials for craftsmen, citizens

and artists than any other nation, - outside of mechanical genius for mere contri-

vance we are not good craftsmen, nor, as good citizens as we should be, nor, are we

artists at all for we are, conciously or unconsciously mastered by our tools.

        To make this assertion clear I offer you, evidence found in the

field of Architecture. It is still a field in which the pulse of the age throbs,

and it is broad enough to represent the errors and possibilities common to our

time. In the past, Architects have embodied the spirit common to their time

in the most noble of noble or records - Buildings. — They have written these

valuable records with the tools at their command and what these records have to

say to us would be insignificant if not wholly illegible it tools suited to

another and a different condition were forced at work to which they were not

fitted

1.
A PHILOSOPHY OF FINE ART.

"The Simplicity of Life lies in one's spirit and attitude of mind", - and it is the expression in the surroundings of one's life, of one's spirit, one's attitude of mind that is realized by means of the Arts. To have an adequate idea of the part Art plays in shaping the characters of men and what it does for the work men do, is to know this expanding,- "blossoming" quality in man's nature- that reaches upward to the spiritual sun for expression as the life principle in the plant reaches toward the more evident but less real sun.

Carlyle gave us a phrasing of a truth, that, (thanks to his good mother) should ring in every boy's head until he grasped its vital meaning and then (thanks to his good wife) be kept still ringing there. Let it serve as a text in connection with our subject.- "The Ideal is within thyself, thy condition is but the stuff thou art to shape that same Ideal out of."

Carlyle meant that the practical is not one thing and the Beautiful another thing; that there is no

"A Philosophy of Fine Art," first read to the University Guild of Evanston, Illinois, 1896, under the original title "The Philosophy of Fine Art." This second draft from 1900 was read to the Chicago Women's Club in 1904.

Typescript of introduction to his German monograph, *Ausgeführte Bauten und
Entwürfe*, published by Ernst Wasmuth in Berlin, 1910; the first draft was written
while residing at the Villino Belvedere in Fiesole, Italy.

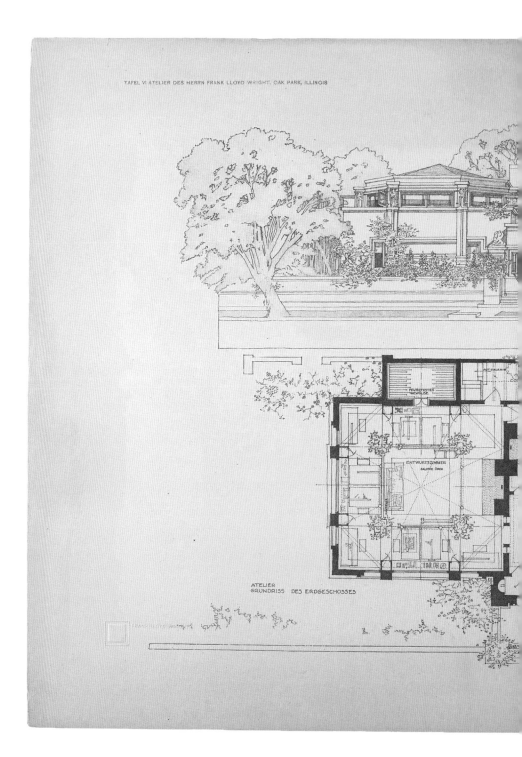

Tafel VI. Atelier des Herrn Frank Lloyd Wright, Oak Park, Illinois, in *Ausgeführte Bauten und Entwürfe*, published by Ernst Wasmuth in Berlin, 1910.

GEDRUCKT UND VERLEGT VON ERNST WASMUTH A.-G., BERLIN

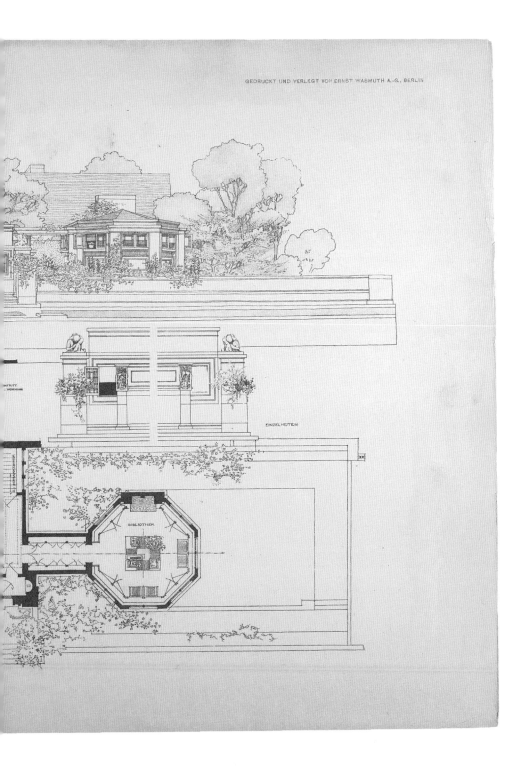

EINTRITT
WOHNUNG

EINZELHEITEN

BIBLIOTHEK

31

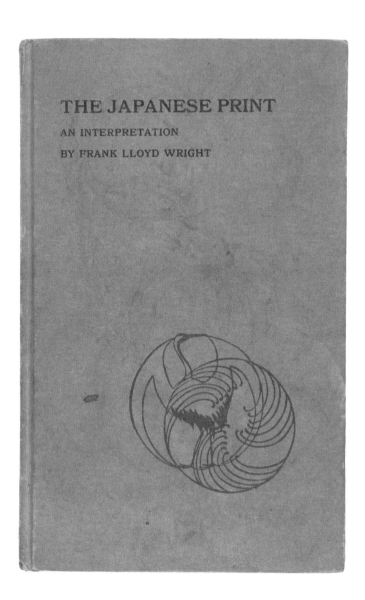

The Japanese Print: An Interpretation, published by Horizon Press in
New York, 1912.

PUBLICATIONS OF THE CITY CLUB OF CHICAGO

CITY RESIDENTIAL LAND DEVELOPMENT

STUDIES IN PLANNING

COMPETITIVE PLANS FOR SUBDIVIDING A TYPICAL
QUARTER SECTION OF LAND IN THE
OUTSKIRTS OF CHICAGO

EDITED BY

ALFRED B. YEOMANS

LANDSCAPE ARCHITECT

THE UNIVERSITY OF CHICAGO PRESS
CHICAGO. ILLINOIS

"Plan by Frank Lloyd Wright," in *City Residential Land Development: Studies in Planning* for the City Club of Chicago competition of 1913, published by University of Chicago Press, 1916.

The New Imperial Hotel in Tokyo: A Message from the Architect, Tokyo, March 24, 1922, in the Japanese science journal *Kagaku Chishiki* (April 1922).

荷稿たるを得るのである。此の原則は不
思ふである。その犯すべからざる原則を恐
るゝが故に、無花果の木に梅の木をつぐ
ことを敢てせないのである。
しかも二つを生ずる原則は共通である。
それは一つである。従って益に吾等が人生
に於て最高の要求として本能的に個性を
認識することは、緊要にして、決して苟
くもすべからざるものである。是を軽視
することは、必ず危険と腐敗とを伴ふの
である。
吾々が、作品、被造物がよく目的と合致
して居るといふことを問題にしたり、
「形」が「用」に即し、「用」が「形」
に即するといふ場合は、則ち此の問題に
触れて居るのである。

見て貫いて、統一の大法といふものが
厳存して居る。そして個性といふものは
むしろ生活の根本を為す精神に對して、
普通の統一性を設揮立するものである。
そして苟くも殺に生きるといふのは、根
本精神を遵奉し保持して行くにあるのだ。
若しこれを疎かにすることあらば、生命
は最早吾等のものでなくなる。そして吾
等の生活はすたれる。

然し此所で、一義の「個」(それは決して
一なる)も、單なる意匠の「個」(それは
單に無智にのみ由來するなる)も種の究
境の値の前には影をひそめなくなると
いふてもその認識は無用である。何とな
れば、その究境の値ひとは人間がその事
業と個性とに於て人生の最高美への「個
は散喜ともなり或は信仰ともなる)の懐
憶によって連せられる堤である。吾々は
「個」に印したがら「個」を越えなけれ
ばならぬ。それはたゞ、原理に服従する
ことによって出来る。

吾々の生るのは、最理の故である。統
一の故である。或は吾人の達し得たる程
度に於て何等かの統一と何等かの本然と
の故である。

「君」の本質は完一である。それこそ實
に本然である。そして其は、見て、有機
的統一あるものに我集されて居る。そし
て生活に於てこの完一の確立すること。
それが生活を有意義ならしめる、其所に
は、買って間に合せるでは許されない、
模倣して親睦するでは許されない、ろく
なものを出さぬ速成では許されない。而
も人間は、超えて此をくりかへして低迷
して居るのである。
世界の國といふ國も、自らの内に發見す
べきものを外に求め、借り物と間に合せ

現代生活の藝術の理想の中心思想とは、
略以上の如くである。そして新帝國ホテ
ルは、その一例である。そしてその然る
所以は深く研究するに値する。
世界は最早や、皮厨の装飾と通り一過の
作品とをこしらへる藝術家に飽き居る。
日本の文明は、今就に以上略説した新し
い意識された理想といふ方面には最も大
な天性を持って居た。但しそれは意識され
て居なかった。若しされて居たら、今更、
失はれたり、見えなくなったりする筈が
ない。若しそれが再び變って來るとすれ
ば、それは苦い經驗と深い内的の闘争を
經て初めて自覺されるであらう。
現今の日本はまさに、悲境である。而も
自分は欺でいふ、日本は自らそれを知ら
ないのだ。

日本の美術は完一性を失って居る。まる
で、感傷的に隠して居る。例へば、劇に
於て、悲劇と思はれて居るものは、質は
悲劇でも何でもない。それはむごたらし
い殺し場だ。そこには、藝性なる何物も
亡ない。自然を欺くかべきへには、種性の
大法の情提の爲めに自分の弱少を揖げる
場合か、その大法の故に自分を亡ぼさね
ばならぬといふ最後の壮嚴にして、つて、
君の人間性が揖接すると云ふことが全然
缺けて居るといふのだ。(大法は人によ
って之を神と呼ぶも防げない。)

日本はまさに、悲境である。特に、君てい
美に對する特有の觀念と完一性に對する
優れたる天性の完璧であったゞけ、それ
だけ更に悲境である。今や日本の足下に
沫れど、嫉疑の如く横はる深淵。――世
界何れの國にか、かつて此の如く危險な
場合に面接したことがある。
日本は小羹を累てゝ大業に就くか。日本
は偏狭と感傷とを棄てるか。感傷的な涙
とは、無智の浪費が熱らずば無盆なる
無智に過ぎないことを知って來くる。
生命を大法にまつて、敬虔にせんと
するか、或は瓢って、日本の特性を軍閥
的卑少にならしむるか。模倣の安卑に頽
れて、無氣力、不敬にならんとするか、
生命を意義あらしる魂も、感能の羈用
に委して頽れ去るが如くならしめんとす
るか。
日本がよく、此の深淵を渡り得たりとす
れば、それは君が日本が自分を見出し、
其を發揮せしめた時である。日本の「個」
の特有なる表現に到達した時である。而
も其「個」は今や盆でない。更に普遍
性に於て深まり、腐まり、更に、自身の

ある、新帝國ホテ□□□、此の規□□下の日
本に對する同情の捧物、――日本の古き
に負ふ所の多い一人の藝術家が、報恩の
意味で日本の建築界に寄與する捧物であ
る。同じく建築に於ける日本の諸見
が、これによって幾何が其の個性を發見
するの一助とならばと覺ひ、
タありき朝ありき、タと朝との別はたゞ
進歩である。
一圏の生命にあっては、一世紀はまさに
一日である。變化は如何に激しくとも最
の進歩は誠に遅々たるものである。日本
にひるがへる膝の日の丸、霊か知る、沈
む夕日か、昇る朝日か。

THE NEW IMPERIAL HOTEL IN TOKYO
A Message From the Architect
Tokyo, March 24, 1922

Art is universal when it is art in the
true sense. All artists are brothers
living or dead. I happen to be an
American architect that is all, just as
my brothers happen to be Japanese or
French or Indian or English architects.

I came to Japan to show how an
organic expression of the ancient spirit
of architecture was possible in new
terms in modern times — not only possible but more alive and warmly related
to life than the cold dead forms Japanese architects go abroad to copy. In
this spirit I have made a building that
looks and feels at home in Japan and
is no mongrel: any study of its parts
in relation to the whole will prove it
thoroughbred.

This building — the New Imperial Hotel
of Tokyo is not designed to be a Japanese building: it is an artist's tribute to
Japan, modern and universal in character.

While there is something Japanese,
Chinese, and of other ancient forms
living in this structure as all may see,
there is neither form, idea, nor pattern
copied from any, ancient or modern.
It is reverent to old Japan, that is all.

In it the most modern conscious ideal
of architecture is living — and that is
the idea of a work of art as beauty
organic or integral — and therefore
working from within outward as contrasted with the idea of art as something applied or put on from the outside
or merely something for its own sake.
There is therefore a fine integrity of
means to ends visible throughout the
structure and a development of parts in
relation to the whole similar to any
consistent expression of nature, like the
trees or a flower. Practical necessities

whole.

Simple materials have been used in
rather easy fashion because character
of the form or idea seemed more important than the quality of texture. In
a building of this size under the circumstances both together could not be had.
Japanese workmen are yet unfamiliar
with masonry and so workmanship is
necessarily crude. Therefore the texture of the building is perhaps coarse
for Japanese taste — more like a woolen
tapestry than a silk brocade: — more
like hand-woven linen than satin. It is
really a gigantic masonry brocade of
brick and stone and copper fused together with concrete inlaid with steel
fibre.

When I agreed to undertake a work
so difficult, so entirely removed from
industrial conditions or methods I knew
I felt that the Japanese people needed
help because they were throwing away
the formes of their old life and bor-
rowing new ones they could not understand: forms already in the scrap-heaps
of the civilizations that produced them.

In all Tokyo there was not a single
building by native or "foreigner" who
really understood the meaning either of
architecture or of what he did in the
name of architecture, nor one that
showed an real love for Japan.

These buildings were bad copies in
bad technique of bad original. The
buildings that were most strange, most
different from old native buildings were
the models of these ugly empty shell
where no spirit of the beautiful could
dwell for a moment.

Japan whose origins reach back into
and are lost in the primitive Chinese
certainly had richer sources of inspiration within herself than any other nation.
Chinese architectures is the most vivid
and noble of all forms of architecture
and this architecture was Japan's in-
heritance.

Japanese architects have betrayed
their country.

During the time I have been engaged
upon this work I have not changed my
mind regarding the needs of Japan but
have abandoned any idea that Japanese
architects realise those needs. They
are learning to do the "foreign thing"
a little better — yes — sometimes doing
it well as in the new Mitsubishi Bank —
a sarcophagus — perfect in propriety in
some land far from Japan. It has,
however, nothing to do with Japan's
case except as a servile obsession, a
mockery. It serves to indicate how
wide of any mark that is her own, her
perceptions are at the present time.

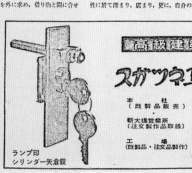

"The New Imperial Hotel in Tokyo: A Message from the Architect, Tokyo,
March 24, 1922," in the Japanese science journal *Kagaku Chishiki* (April 1922).

IN THE CAUSE OF ARCHITECTURE

By Frank Lloyd Wright

1. THE LOGIC OF THE PLAN

Plan! There is something elemental in the word itself. A pregnant plan has logic—is the logic of the building squarely stated. Unless it is the plan for a foolish Fair.

A good plan is the beginning and the end, because every good plan is organic. That means that its development in all directions is inherent—inevitable.

Scientifically, artistically to foresee all is "to plan." There is more beauty in a fine ground plan than in almost any of its ultimate consequences.

In itself it will have the rhythms, masses and proportions of a good decoration if it is the organic plan for an organic building with individual style—consistent with materials.

All is there seen—purpose, materials, method, character, style. The plan? The prophetic soul of the building—a building that can live only because of the prophecy that is the plan. But it is a map, a chart, a mere diagram, a mathematical projection before the fact and, as we all have occasion to know, accessory to infinite crimes.

To judge the architect one need only look at his ground plan. He is master then and there, or never. Were all elevations of the genuine buildings of the world lost and the ground plans saved, each building would construct itself again. Because before the plan is a plan it is a concept in some creative mind. It is, after all, only a purposeful record of that dream which saw the destined building living in its appointed place. A dream—but precise and practical, the record to be read by the like-minded.

The original plan may be thrown away as the work proceeds—probably most of those for the most wonderful buildings in the world were, because the concept grows and matures during realization, if the master-mind is continually with the work. But that plan had, first, to be made. Ultimately it should be corrected and recorded.

But to throw the plans away is a luxury ill afforded by the organizations of our modern method. It has ruined owners and architects and enriched numberless contractors. Therefore conceive the building in the imagination, not on paper but in the mind, thoroughly—before touching paper. Let it live there—gradually taking more definite form before committing it to the draughting board. When the thing lives for you— start to plan it with tools. Not before. To draw during conception or "sketch," as we say, experimenting with practical adjustments to scale, is well enough if the concept is clear enough to be firmly held. It is best to cultivate the imagination to construct and complete the building before working upon it with T square and triangle. Working on it with triangle and T square should modify or extend or intensify or test the conception—complete the harmonious adjustment of its parts. But if the original concept is lost as the drawing proceeds, throw all away and begin afresh. To throw away a concept entirely to make way for a fresh one—that is a faculty of the mind not easily cultivated. Few have that capacity. It is perhaps a gift—but may be attained by practice. What I am trying to express is that the plan must start as a truly creative matter and mature as such. All is won or lost before anything more tangible begins.

"In the Cause of Architecture: I. The Logic of the Plan," in *Architectural Record*, vol. 63, no. 1 (January 1928): 49–57. Editor M. A. Mikkelsen commissioned Wright to write a series of fourteen essays for *Architectural Record* all under the same heading, "In the Cause of Architecture."

1930–1932

At the age of sixty-three, Frank Lloyd Wright entered the 1930s in a state of involuntary retirement. While his private life had stabilized, he was virtually devoid of work, partially as a consequence of the Wall Street Crash of 1929. To add insult to injury, 1929 also saw the publication of Henry-Russell Hitchcock's *Modern Architecture: Romanticism and Reintegration*, in which Hitchcock relegated Wright to the category of the New Tradition, along with such seemingly *retarditaire* architects as Ragnar Östberg, the designer of the Stockholm Town Hall. Clearly this did not sit well with Wright, and his unpublished "Poor Little American Architecture" [page 46] was the start of a rebarbative relationship with Hitchcock—one that assumed an ad hominem character in 1932, before being repaired through the magnanimity of Hitchcock's critical acumen, namely, his 1943 *In the Nature of Materials* dedicated to Wright's work. Despite his refusal to be counted among the New Traditionalists, Wright nonetheless affirmed his perennial anti-avant-gardist stance when he wrote, "...all that is valuable in either Tradition or Pioneering is Old in the New and New in the Old."

In 1930, Wright gave his Kahn lectures at Princeton University under the rubric of "modern" rather than organic architecture. Over the course of six sessions, Wright presented a summation of his thought as it had evolved over the previous three decades. In the first two lectures addressed to the problem of arriving at an authentic environmental culture for a democratic, industrialized society, Wright began with a reformulation of his 1901 address "The Art and Craft of the Machine," and went on in Semperian terms to decry a proclivity for the mass-production and cheap substitution of both material and form. Wright was particularly scathing in this regard about the wholesale manufacture of fake antique furniture expressly reproduced for the reassurance of a deracinated *arriviste* middle class that had lost its original identity. For Wright, the model for an alternative machine-age culture lay in the architecture of the Momoyama era of Japan, and to this end he stressed its standardized modularity, its compatibility with nature, its respect for the intrinsic character of material, its integral ornamentation, and above all its elimination of insignificant form.

In his second lecture, "Style in Industry" [page 47], Wright insisted on the generic character of the term rather than on "styles" in an academic sense. He outlined a hypothetical program for a new school of industrial art that was eventually realized, in a much more modified form, in the Taliesin Fellowship. Wright modeled the first version of this program on the 1901 Darmstadt Künstlerkolonie, even including the appointment of seven "elect" artists who could offer instruction in their respective crafts — treating with wood, glass, metals, textiles, and pottery, etc. While landscape and urbanism were to be added to the curriculum, architecture as such was inexplicably omitted. That such a school was in the process of being inaugurated at Cranbrook, near Detroit, under the leadership of Eliel Saarinen, surely accounts for the subsequent friendly rivalry between Saarinen and Wright.

The Kahn lectures establish beyond any doubt that Wright was always well-informed about what was happening in Europe; for in addition to his familiarity with the Wiener Werkstätte and his appreciation for the best of French Art Deco, Wright was fully cognizant of the work of Le Corbusier, his nemesis in so many respects. Thus Wright's deprecation of the fake classical cornice in his third lecture parallels to the letter Le Corbusier's own antipathy to classical moldings, whereas in his next lecture, "The Cardboard House" [page 48], he took issue with the form and substance of Le Corbusier's Purist villas, arguing all too knowingly that "...they are the superficial badly built product of this superficial new 'surface-mass' aesthetic, falsely claiming French painting as a parent." Equally opposed to Le Corbusier's Ville Contemporaine of 1922 as to his slogan, "a house is a machine for living in," Wright opted for the dissolution of cities and for the redistribution of the population over the countryside in his final lecture. This general thesis, echoing Soviet deurbanization theories from exactly the same period, came to be fully elaborated in his Broadacre City of 1934, categorically anti-Classic and pro-Gothic and discriminating in this broad opposition between the cult of the pictorial versus the tactility of architecture. Wright argued that the figurative representational arts should be subsumed under the new arts of photography and film. In a similar vein, he predicated his antitheses of the bourgeois city on the universalization of power and information—prophetic in this regard about the ubiquitous triumph of electrification and television. Thus while Wright was anti-avant-gardist he was certainly not opposed to the process of modernization when it appeared to resolve the intractable problems of the epoch. As in his 1931 lecture "To a Young Man in Architecture" [page 49], Wright saw the future in terms of an industrial process that could still be symbolically inflected. As he put it in the first Kahn lecture, "The machine does not write the doom of liberty, but is waiting at man's hand as a peerless tool, for him to use, to put a foundation beneath a genuine democracy."

Started in 1927 at his wife Olgivanna's urging, when Wright was sixty-three, Wright's An Autobiography—first published in 1932 and again in amplified form in 1943—was by far the longest text he ever wrote. [pages 50–57] There is more than a hint in the opening lines of each of the three books from which the first edition was composed that Wright would have liked to have structured the whole thing around a seasonal theme. The winter, spring, and summer sequence implies an autumn that would not come to pass for Wright, who, in actuality, outlived the first edition by another twenty-seven years, before he finally succumbed in the spring of 1959 at the age of ninety-two.

Much of the autobiography is given over to what Wright called "friction, waste and slip," a period of almost twenty years, 1909 to 1928, when he was constantly pursued by women, lawyers, creditors, clients, press photographers, and newspapermen. The somewhat rambling record of this period, some of which, if we are to believe him, was dictated on the run, is as revealing for its asides as for its prejudices—not to mention the long discursive passages that from time to time interrupt the narrative with reflections of substance. However, the omissions, too, are revealing, since these imply various Freudian lapses, ranging from Wright's Oedipal relationship with his mother to his narcissistic habit of failing to give credit where credit was due. This even applies to the engineer Paul Mueller, without whom Wright could never have achieved his Prairie masterworks, from the Larkin Building to the Imperial Hotel in Tokyo. Although Mueller is sympathetically rendered throughout the text, he surely deserves as much if not more credit for the survival of the hotel in the 1923 Tokyo earthquake.

In one way or another the autobiography serves to confirm many key facts that one always suspected about Wright or of which one had been made aware by other writers, at other times—even by Wright himself. Thus one learns again of his youthful reading of Victor Hugo's *Notre Dame de Paris*; the famous phrase *ceci tuera cela* ("this will kill that") with which Hugo alluded to the invention of movable type and to the concomitant rise of the media and the decline of architecture. Wright's reaction to this prophecy was somewhat ironic given that he was to become a media figure and that he wrote more than any other architect, with the possible exception of Le Corbusier.

We are repeatedly reminded of Wright's distance from European modernism, be it in art, music, or architecture. He even went so far as to liken modern music to the discordant sounds produced at the musical evenings of his Oak Park family, and later he compared the playful assembly of his daughter's colored building blocks to the abstract creations of modern art. In 1943, he extended his critique of the European avant-garde by boldly proclaiming his antipathy to Le Corbusier and insisting elsewhere that the entire body of Cubism and Futurism was predicated on the Japanese print. In retrospect this seems a trifle perverse, given that he later became Hilla Rebay's architect for Solomon R. Guggenheim's collection of non-objective art. Yet Wright was more anti-avant-garde than he was anti-modern, as we may judge from the House on the Mesa (1931) or Fallingwater (1935). Thus he ironically depicted himself Americanizing Europe while the European moderns were busy Europeanizing America.

Wright constantly displayed his background as a nineteenth-century romanticist, not to mention the Midwestern provincialism from which he never quite escaped. Indeed, the egocentricity of much of the text owes a great deal to Wright's "lieber meister," Louis Sullivan, and above all to Sullivan's *The Autobiography of an Idea*, published in 1926. In that posthumous publication, as in Wright's autobiography, the "idea" turns out to be a retrospective of the view of the author himself as a predestined genius. That Wright elected to see his life in this way is suggested in Book One by the idealized account of his bucolic boyhood in Spring Green, Wisconsin—the Usonian agrarian idyll of the "God Almighty Lloyd-Jones's" to whom Wright was the prodigal son.

Wright, like Sullivan, was destined to assume the role of the redeeming genius perennially misunderstood by the "mobocracy," as Wright contemptuously referred to the American public in his gloss on Sullivan's ornament, entitled *Genius and the Mobocracy* of 1949. As we know, Wright, like Sullivan, believed in the emancipatory myth of American democracy and in the manifest destiny of the post-industrial age. However, going beyond Sullivan's technological rationalism and the romantic pathos of his compensatory symbolic ornament, Wright pursued nothing less than a totally new beginning, politically and otherwise. To this end, he championed the single tax theory of Henry George.[1] For Wright, electrification, mechanized agriculture, and Taylorized products were each portents favoring a totally new symbiotic synthesis with nature that on one occasion he elected to call "organic plasticity." He saw this last as an infinitely extendable horizontal civilization, following the groundline of his mythical prairie. Wright believed, as few have either before or since, that architecture was a crusade on the behalf of human civilization rather than a mere profession. That this life-long passion caused Wright to write of his work with unmatched elegance and conviction is evident from the following passage describing the 1923 Millard House, also known as La Minitura, in Pasadena:

> La Miniatura happened as the cactus grown, in that region sill showing what folk from the Middle-Western prairies did when, inclined to quit, the prosperous came loose and rolled down there into that far corner to bask in eternal sunshine.
>
> Near by, that arid, sunlit strand is still unspoiled desert. You may see what a poetic thing this land was before this homely mid-west invasion. Curious tan-gold foothills rise from tattooed sand-stretches to join slopes spotted as the leopard-skin with grease-bush. This foreground spreads to distances so vast — human scale is utterly lost as all features recede, turn blue, recede and become bluer still to merge their blue mountain shapes, snow-capped, with the azure of the skies. The one harmonious note man has introduced into these vast perspectives, aside from the long, low plastered wall, is the eucalyptus tree. Tall, tattered ladies, these trees stand with careless feminine grace in the charming abandon appropriate to perpetual sunshine, adding beauty to the olive-green and ivory-white of an exotic symphony in silvered gold and rose-purple. Water comes, but it comes as a deluge once a year to surprise the roofs, sweep the sands into ripples and roll boulders along in the gashes combed by sudden streams in the sands of the desert. Then — all dry as before.[2]

Despite such lyrical evocations, invariably inspired by a strong feeling for natural landscape, the lasting fascination of Wright's autobiography stemmed unavoidably from its confessional character, with which he both revealed and concealed errors and omissions of his life. As he put it with admirable candor:

> Listen to any man you meet and you will see that nothing is more natural than autobiography, and usually, nothing more tedious. Every man you meet is either intensely, modestly, offensively, or charmingly autobiographical. Women are less so. They have learned the wisdom that makes them natural biographers. Too often, ones.

Thus Book Two, dedicated to Wright's apprenticeship in Chicago, displays his racial prejudices as much as it admits to his psychological dependency on the Prairie School as a whole, not to mention Daniel Burnham's generous offer to send Wright to the École des Beaux-Arts; an offer, needless to say, that Wright refused. Elsewhere his spunky character comes fully to the fore in the temerity with which he built the sixty-foot-high windmill tower Romeo and Juliet for his doting aunts in 1896, seven years after he assisted them with the building of the Hillside Home School in 1887, when he was only twenty-years-old.

Despite his gratitude to Sullivan for his apprenticeship, "as a pencil in the hand of the master," many of Wright's own protégés are summarily eclipsed in this account, from Walter Burley Griffin, who was Wright's top assistant during the formative years of the Prairie Style, to Griffin's wife Marion Mahony, who was without doubt Wright's most brilliant delineator and to whom Wright sensibly first offered the management of his studio when he decamped to Europe with Mamah Borthwick Cheney in 1909. This convenient amnesia extends beyond his most intimate colleagues to such collaborators as Jens Jensen, the Chicago landscapist with whom he worked on the garden of the Avery Coonley House, and the Czech Antonin Raymond, who went with Wright to Tokyo to work on the Imperial Hotel. Even his own architect son John Lloyd is patronizingly presented as his father's faithful site architect. Of his eldest son, Lloyd Wright, we learn nothing at all, despite the fact that he helped his father in his Fiesole exile by drafting the illustrations for the Wasmuth volumes. Understandably enough, perhaps, Wright was more generous to his clients, to the men who trusted him, to the good old boys, and, for that matter, to his distinguished patrons of the opposite sex, such as the strong-willed Aline Barnsdall and the cultivated Mrs. George Millard. Above all he fully acknowledged Darwin D. Martin, who was a client and loyal supporter throughout his life.

Strong women clearly played a major role in Wright's life: from his mother, who was a doting and willful presence until she died at eighty-four in 1923, when Wright himself was in his fifty-sixth year, to the hypersensitive and demanding Miriam Noel who married him in 1923 after nine distressful years, and who unadvisedly intervened in Wright's life soon after the death of the radical feminist and ill-fated Mrs. Cheney, who was possibly the most intense passion of Wright's life. Notably she is referred to but never mentioned by name. Thus he alluded to her as a figure of fate, "who by force of rebellion as by way of love was then implicated with me," and later he justified her unmarked Taliesin grave with the words, "Why mark the spot where desolation ended and began?" Destined to outlive him by twenty-six years was Olgivanna (born Olga Ivanova Lazovich), whom Wright met in 1924, when she was a soon-to-be divorcé and committed follower of George Gurdjieff. After his marriage to her, in 1928, she succeeded in totally reorganizing his life and indeed his means of livelihood by starting the Taliesin Fellowship, subjected to her spiritual guidance. At its best the Fellowship was a unique cultural institution capable of providing an ad hoc education as well as affording a unique form of apprenticeship; at its worst (and the experience varied), it was somewhat exploitative. Displaying a strength of a very different kind, there was also Wright's first wife, Catherine Tobin, who clearly was a source of nurture and much support during the first decade of Wright's Prairie practice, 1894 to 1909.

Of this formative period, the autobiography is reasonably forthcoming, except for certain masterworks such as the Larkin Building, the Avery Coonley House, and the Robie House, of which we learn little. We learn even less of his twenty-four-story skyscraper designed for San Francisco in 1912, since it is inexplicably absent from the account. Needless to say he expanded at length on the virtues of the Prairie Style as opposed to what he regarded as the "monogaria" of the American suburb, including even that of his beloved Oak Park, with its Gothic carpenter's jiggerwork, "little painted cardboard lawns and candle snuffer roof," its pernicious practice of building basements, dormers, bay windows, and its fatal weakness for the Arts and Crafts decadence of English stockbrokers' s Tudor—to which even he once succumbed in order to remain in practice in his Moore House built in Oak Park in 1895.

Amid the reiteration of Wright's organic Prairie principles, two things strike one particularly forcibly. The first is his aversion to the ornate portico of the average suburban house, an aversion that no doubt explains his preference for the half-hidden side entries of almost all his domestic works. The second is his mythical, one might even say personal, obsession with fire, of which he wrote, "It comforted me to see the fire burning deep in the solid masonry of the house itself. A feeling that came to stay." Of equal consequence in this regard is his direct admission, in all but Semperian terms, that he was "working away at the wall as a wall and bringing it towards the function of a screen." Part and parcel of this dematerialization was Wright's advocacy of the casement instead of the guillotine sash window, because it opened out and thereby dissolved the barrier between interior and exterior. Along with his deployment of the casement *en serie* was his preference for low, overhanging, gutterless eaves, which when painted white reflected light into the house interior and were attractive to him for their spontaneous generation of icicles in winter. Complementary to all this was Wright's newfound sense of plasticity, what he referred to as "streamlining," which entailed the cantilever, the lateral penetration of space, and the elimination of fittings and all the other knickknacks, including artworks of dubious quality.

Following Wright's first meeting with his client Aline Barnsdall in 1915, Wright's sensibility began to be transformed by a confrontation with the Californian desert, which by virtue of its hot dry climate became the setting and inspiration for such structures as the canvas-covered Ocotilla Camp built in the Arizona desert in 1927. The same dry, earth-colored landscape led to his atomization of tectonic form first appearing as the textile concrete block mosaic of the Millard House, La Miniatura. From these two related but different structural approaches—one may think of them as framed dematerialization versus piled-up materiality—came Wright's obsession with hermetic screen walls built of tessellated con-crete, copper, or glass, or of a judicious mixture of these materials, as in his National Life Insurance Company offices designed for the "business mystic" A.M. Johnson. It is of utmost significance that Wright conceived of himself as a weaver rather than a sculptor and that woven fabric would be the metaphor for all of his architecture, from the high point of the Prairie Style through the SC Johnson Administration Building, completed for Hibbard Johnson in Racine, Wisconsin in 1938. This vast mushroom-columned, lily-pad hall Wright saw as "an inspiring place to work as any cathedral was a place to worship."

How Wright managed to write as much as he did and how, despite receiving major commissions in the mid-1930s, this literary output con-tinued unabated until the last years of his life, remains something of a mystery. Wright's proclivity in this regard not only testifies to the quite exceptional range of his talent, but also to the soundness of the basic education that he received under the supervision of his ever-watchful mother. More important perhaps, given his subsequent resistance to formal education, it points to the scope of Wright's self-cultivation, ardently pursued throughout his life. From this surely came his extensive vocabulary, his sense of rhythm, and his remarkable command of metaphor and simile that accorded his texts a rich, if ornate, precision. In the second edition of his autobiography he cited the authors to whom he felt indebted. This list is revealing not only for its catholic scope, but also for its idiosyncratic juxtapositions. Thus we find the Russian anarchosocialist Peter Kropotkin close to the Danish Christian revolutionary theologian Nicolaj Grundtvig, the late American social theorist Thorstein Veblen in the same line as the pioneering psychologist Arnold Gesell. Strangely enough, given the circumstances under which this edition was written, there is no mention of Gurdjieff. Despite his anarchic nature and his susceptibility to romance and mysticism, Wright's larger view was politically radical. In this however, like Le Corbusier, he was inclined towards the ambiguous progressive right, rather than to the left.

Notes

1. Henry George, *Progress and Poverty* (Garden City, NY: Doubleday, Page & Co., 1879).

2. Frank Lloyd Wright, *An Autobiography* (New York: Longmans, Green & Co, 1932), 239.

POOR LITTLE AMERICAN ARCHITECTURE

Safely tucked away by Henry Russell Hitchcock, in my own little red square, as the greatest architect of the first one-quarter (to be precise) of the Nineteenth Century, I cock an eye at him, - wondering--(strange name that for a Frenchman!)

Nor do I know ~~the~~ *Russell* Hitchcock. But not long since dropping into the offices of The Architectural Record on business concerning a book-(I am, I believe, the last "prolific writer" on Architecture in the whole world, to attempt one,) I casually picked up a black engraving of a man: hat, ~~the~~ typical French Mansard, beard, French, although the young woman at the desk, (her smile ~~was~~ most engaging) ~~said~~ *volunteered that -* the actual color of the beard was not typically French.

That is how I learned what Henry ~~Russell~~ Hitchcock looked like and all I know about him except that I have been told ~~that~~ *Russell* occasionally comes over from Paris to teach young ladies at Vassar what they should think about Architecture, and that he is addicted to photographs for criticism. So I am as qualified to write about him as he is to write about me. I know him by a black engraving *casually picked up* and his ~~writings~~ *aesthetics*. He knows me by *probably picked up as casually - bad,* some bad photographs of my work, because there have never been any other kind, and *taken off my work* knows me, too, perhaps - I doubt it- by some "pieces" I have tried to write *that would* *I doubt it because he doesn't seem to be the kind of man* *care to heed anything any one else wrote on his especial subject.* Two things I gather. ~~from what I have seen.~~ First: Mr. Hitchcock is a man of decided opinions. Second: he is the man to keep ~~his~~ opinions right there where they are. In reading Mr. Hitchcock's book, therefore, one is inevitably concerned with Mr. Hitchcock's inveterate opinions. Fortunately for him ~~this~~ *recently achieved aesthetic* his ~~author~~ needs no conception of Architecture. In his own opinion, certain of his opinions are prophetic and he wishes to keep them that way, *that is all.*

"Poor Little American Architecture," 1930.

Toleration and Liberty are the foundation of the great Republic.
Liberty in Art as well as liberty in Society should be the offspring
of political liberty.

For a New people a New Art.

~~Toleration and liberty are the foundations of the great Republic~~

Now let the artist come to has a public.
And as seen in Machinery Materials and Men, he now has the
acting and means — again

For our text in connection with Style in Industry suppose we go
for back again in History — to the birth of old Japan — and take —

"An artists limitations are his best friends"

At least the unique civilization of history from Jimmu Tenno of pendulous island as it
arises from the sea in the swirls of perpetual winter and goes all the
way South to perpetual Summer affords best proof of the truth to be
found on this Earth.

In Jimmu's Island — there was perfect Style in Industry until
Nippon was discovered by the pattern range of commo due Perry's guns.
Probably. No — Certainly by the arts and crafts as they developed in Japan
during her centuries of isolation and happy concentration afford an object
lessons in Style —. Industry and Style were nonmeaning terms —
and both supremely as natural. Native in true sense. There was no
separate and contrasted existence there between Art and Nature
And one can nowhere do so well by ourselves in consideration of
this matter of Style in our own automatic industries and conclude
upon automatic acquiesce of men instead of their crafts manship
than by giving attention to the ease and naturalness with which
these Japanese achieve style.
The best now is to educate designers instead of making crafts men for Our
crafts men are prolific, ubiquitous in fact — efficient beyond worlds so
for us then go, power stripped to the bone. Well, or one thing
to get them work to do that they may do well. Instil into
the essential "designers" as possible the principles which made the art and
Craft of old Japan a living thing. Japan —
Get them in touch with art and craft influence it had similar truth of
being and force in effect enable them to learn the secrets of cause and effect in work and materials in relation to
Life. — the line — in a way we differ. We line and our souls have much
in common with all souls — the principles therefore on which we
must work on Style for ourselves will not change — Our applications
will — of course — change — will be simpler, broader — more a matter
of textures and sublimated mathematics. as music in the days of ancient handicraft.
Our applications will be more

THE CARD-BOARD HOUSE

Princeton - May 14, 1930

By Frank Lloyd Wright
Taliesin
Spring Green
Wisconsin

"The Cardboard House," one of the six Kahn Lectures at Princeton University, delivered on May 14, 1930.

TO THE YOUNG MAN IN ARCHITECTURE.

" Chicago Institute, of Art Lecture- ~~Goodman Theatre~~- October 1st.

Art *Afternoon* *; Fullerton Hall.*

The new architecture

By. Frank Lloyd Wright,
Taliesin, Spring Green
Wisconsin.

"To The Young Man in Architecture," one of two lectures delivered at the Art
Institute of Chicago, October 1, 1930. Published in *Two Lectures on Architecture*
by the Art Institute of Chicago, 1931; the draft held by the Avery Library includes
a note from Wright stating "The New Architecture."

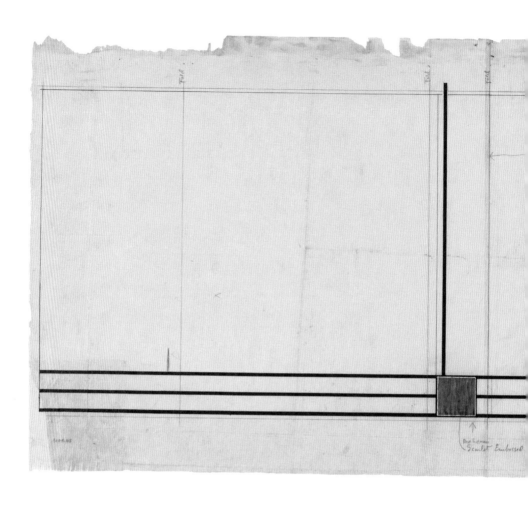

50 Early design sketches for *An Autobiography,* circa 1931. The first edition was divided into three books: "Book One: Family, Fellowship;" "Book Two: Work;" and "Book Three: Freedom." For the final cover of the book see page 96.

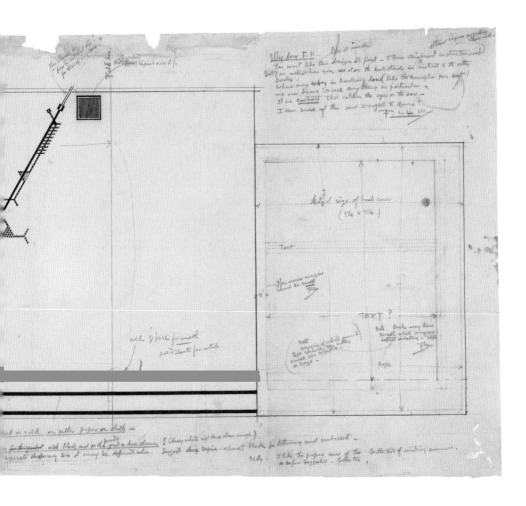

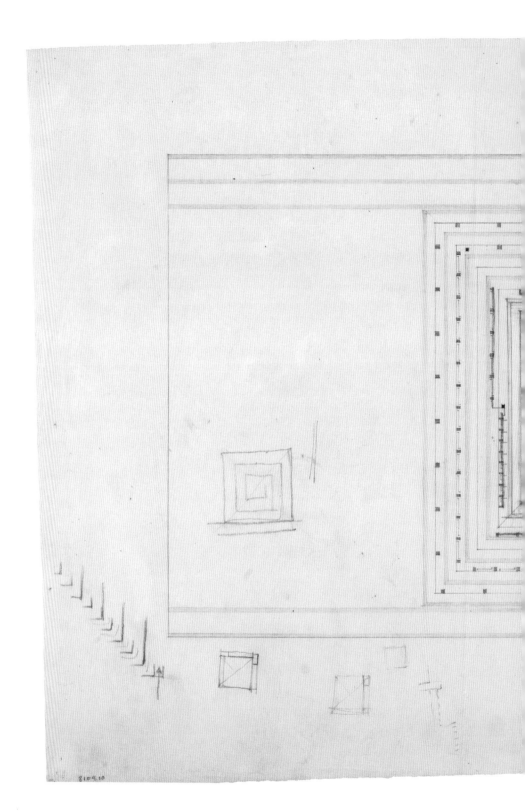

52 An early study titled "From Generation to Generation," which eventually became "Book Two: Work." For a later version see page 55.

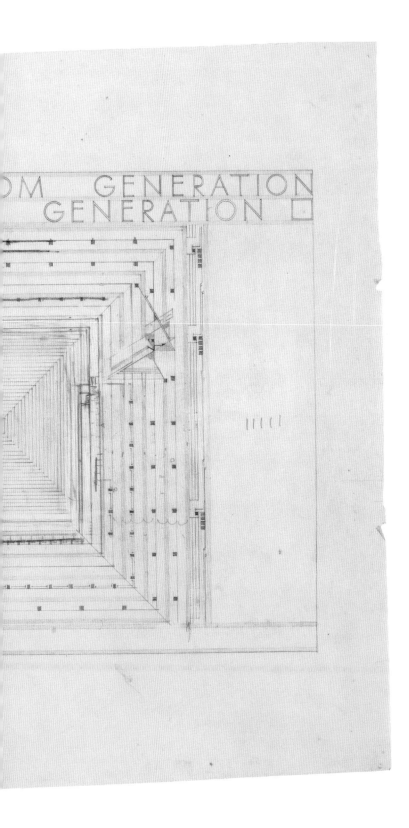

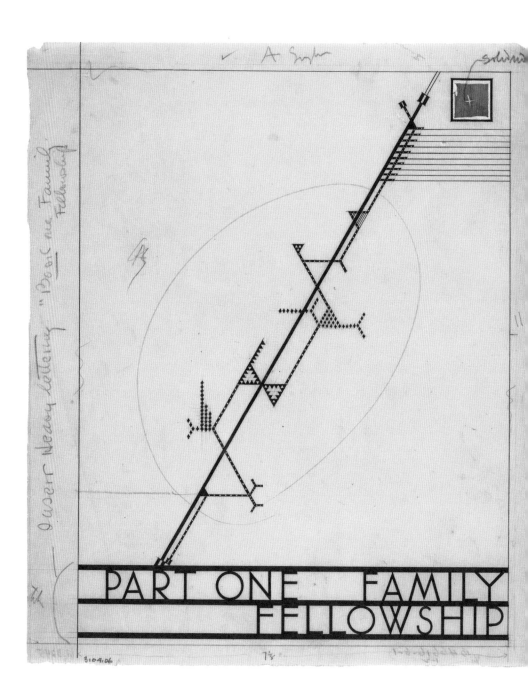

Draft of the divider page for "Book One: Family, Fellowship." In the second edition of *An Autobiography*, Wright divided this chapter into two parts.

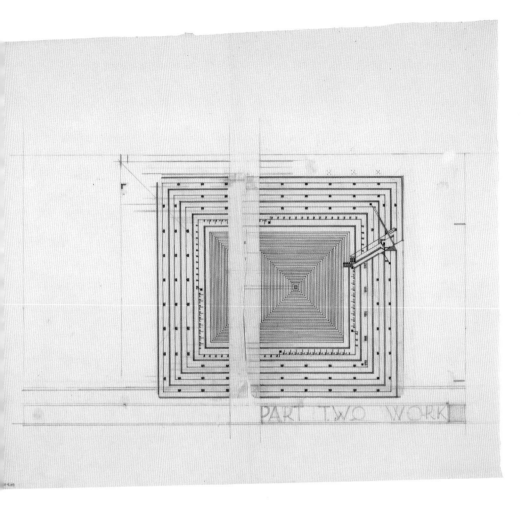

A later study of the divider page for the second book, "Book Two: Work."

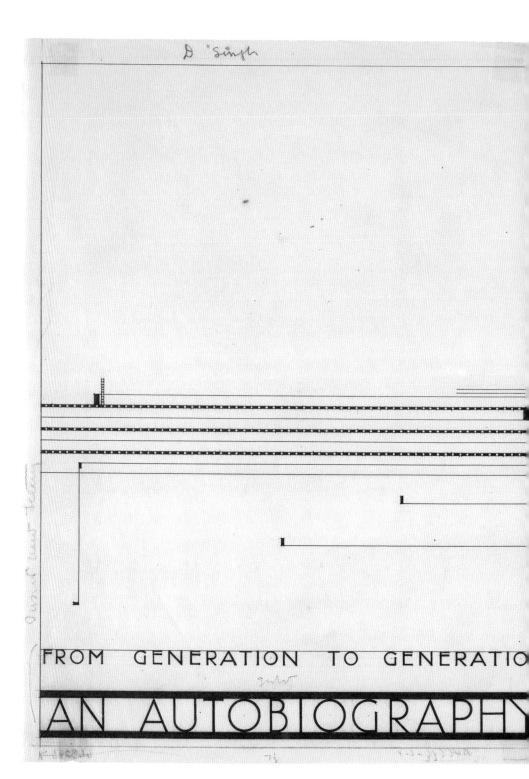

D 'singh

FROM GENERATION TO GENERATIO

AN AUTOBIOGRAPHY

Detailed full-spread mockup of third book title page, "Book Three: Freedom."

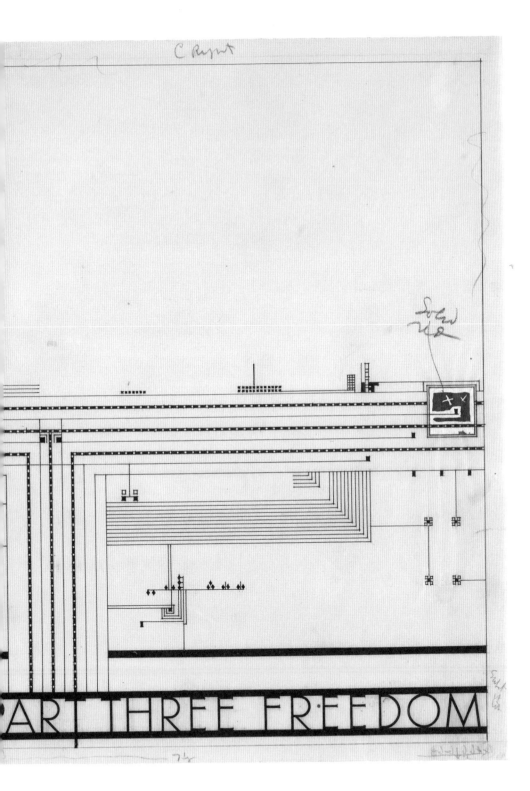

PART THREE FREEDOM

1931–1939

The publication of his autobiography and, shortly afterwards, the foundation of the Taliesin Fellowship brought Wright at the age of sixty-five to a new threshold in life, not only because he found himself without work in the aftermath of the Wall Street Crash of 1929 but also because he had to confront an entirely different situation from the one in which he had worked at the turn of the century. Now Wright had to recognize his Midwestern isolation in the picturesque but provincial landscape of his beloved Wisconsin and the emergence of a new architectural situation, which ironically enough was largely due to his own influence, as disseminated through the Wasmuth portfolios of his executed projects. All of this is evident from his essays of the early 1930s, beginning with a typical complaint about the way he had been misunderstood by Europeans, who had, in his view, already taken his reformist zeal too far and turned it into a kind of stripped abstraction that he abhorred—as he put it in his first essay of 1931, the cult of "the straight line and the flat plane." Who he had in mind, of course, were all those avant-garde practitioners of the International Style, a term that he seemed to have coined prior to its adoption by Henry-Russell Hitchcock and Philip Johnson.

This was not the only change he had to confront, however; for apart from the abstractions of the European avant-garde, there were anathemas closer to home: the emergence of the mega-skyscraper, as exemplified by the Chrysler Building of 1929, and the transformation of the American

Beaux-Arts tradition into the compromise of the modernistic Art Deco, a monumental ornamental manner that was obviously somewhat too close to home as far as Wright was concerned, although he never admitted it. Thus the early 1930s found him railing against two different manifestations: first, the Parisian Exposition Internationale des Arts Décoratifs of 1925 that had brought legitimacy to what he called "the *Mexicano* manner;" and second, the forthcoming "Century of Progress" exhibition scheduled to open in Chicago in 1933, a Midwestern fête from which Wright had been pointedly excluded. One of the main figures in all this was the then-Art Deco master Raymond Hood, about whom Wright felt ambivalent but freely admitted was a man of talent, wit, and charm.

However, architecturally speaking, Hood was also anathema to Wright, as was architect Joseph Urban, who was largely responsible for the Babylonian manner of the "Century of Progress" exhibition: a floodlit, theatrical display that Wright saw as exploiting the vulgar sensibility of the mobocracy. Caught in the Depression between the Scylla and Charybdis of popular American taste, Wright could stand neither the neo-colonialism of middle America, as was then being sponsored by the federal government, nor the pseudo-modern, El Dorado manner of Jazz Moderne. At the same time he could not align himself with what he regarded as the "neutered" manner of European functionalism, particularly as this was then being propagated by the Museum of Modern Art, New York under the curatorial guidance of Hitchcock, Johnson, and Alfred Barr. By way of compensating for having accepted this critical patronage, Wright would continue to denigrate the tyros of the East Coast throughout the 1930s. What irked Wright the most was that they were the only figures aside from Lewis Mumford who recognized the continuing importance of his contribution. This explains the awkward explanation that he felt he had to make with regard to his participation in the 1932 MoMA exhibition. Perhaps the most surprising thing about his self-serving anti-apology is the fact that, notwithstanding his pan-German affinities, he regarded Oswald Spengler as the ultimate neutering demiurge of the Western avant-garde, as per his essay "Of Thee I Sing," published in *Shelter* magazine, April 1932 [page 71]:

> I know the European neuter's argument: The Western soul is dead; Western intelligence, though keen, is therefore sterile and can realize an impression but not expression of life except as life may be recognized as some intellectual formula. . . We are sickened by capitalistic centralization but not so sick, I believe, that we need not confess impotence

by embracing a communistic exterior discipline in architecture to kill finally what spontaneous life we have left to circumstance... So we need no *Geist der Kleinlichkeit* touting a style at us. No, Herr Spengler, we are not yet impotent.[1]

Here once more, we encounter the implication that the curators of the 1932 MoMA show were, with their *Sachlich* taste, quintessentially asexual, aside from the even greater sin of including Raymond Hood in the show.

Sequestered in a country that in his view was economically and spiritually bankrupt, Wright focused his critical acumen on one target after another—first on Hood for taking "a heavy header into the blood and thunder mass known as *modernism*," second on Albert Kahn "for putting on the architecture" in his nonindustrial work, and finally on Hood's RCA building, which between the lines one feels Wright ultimately envied. The first break from this constant carping came with the prospectus "The Hillside Home School of Allied Arts" [page 72]. This, the most substantial text of 1931, throws an intriguing light on Wright's promise to his then deceased aunts, Jane and Ellen Lloyd Jones, to reopen that abandoned Hillside Home School, which he had built for them in 1902. Wright's intent was to restore the existing ruin and turn it into a school for applied art, featuring classes in architecture, painting, poetry, sculpture, glass and metal work, dance, and drama. This curriculum and its financial prospectus was painstakingly elaborated on, and at one time looked as if it would be sponsored by the University of Wisconsin. However, support was not forthcoming and one year later the Wrights shifted their energy to a similar proposal under a different name, namely the more modest program of the Taliesin Fellowship. "The Hillside Home School of the Allied Arts" thus became the first draft of the Taliesin Fellowship prospectus, which was cast in a number of different versions between 1932 and 1933. In an early draft, however, Wright entered a mea culpa plea made on behalf of the American people:

> We have no superstructure, that is to say no culture above the matters of behavior, commerce, industry, politics, and an unsure taste for *objets d'art*...
> We are a nation rich beyond the bounds, even of our own avarice, living in abundance with a creature-comfort undreamed of in the World before. We are ingenious, inventive, scientifically, commercially progressive and, as the whole World has occasion to know—uncreative... Nor will more than three-fifths of our people know what is meant by the assertion that the American is "uncreative."[2]

However, coincidentally, Wright's Hillside Home School prospectus was in part a response to the challenge of Finnish architect Eliel Saarinen, who after a decade as resident architect and ideologue was in 1932 appointed director of the newly founded Cranbrook Art Academy in Bloomfield Hills, Michigan. Wright had been nursing a similar idea for some time as his 1928 *Architectural Record* series, "In the Cause of Architecture," makes clear. Certainly it had been in the back of his mind ever since the first *Gesamtkunstwerk* triumph of his early career: namely, the realization of Midway Gardens, when he had a number of different artists collaborating under his direction. The Hillside Home School prospectus had its students studying all branches of applied and fine art while at the same time earning their keep through communal construction and agrarian work, thereby sustaining Wright's self-subsistent Arts and Crafts, land-based economy. Wright also envisaged augmenting this rustic *modus vivendi* by selling the artworks produced in the school:

> Thus belonging to the school would be each month a very considerable product of modern beautifully useful or usefully beautiful things ready for markets and influence. Stuffs, tapestries, table linens, new cotton fabrics, batik, with special emphasis on tapestries, table glassware, glass flower holders, lighting devices of glass, and glass dishes of all sorts, ashtrays, window glass, and glass mosaics, necklaces, decorative beads, and objects of glass.[3]

However, this was not the only feature that the prospective Hillside Home School would have shared with its German predecessor, the Bauhaus. For both institutions would eventually attach great importance to music, drama, and dance. Above all, in Wright's case, Wagner's music-drama was the ultimate vehicle for the total work of art.

Surprisingly enough, given his Arts and Crafts bias, Wright entered into the subject of town planning in his curriculum for the Hillside Home School; and this was the theme to which he returned in his book *The Disappearing City* of 1932 [page 73] (initially drafted under the title *The Industrial Revolution Runs Away*). Wright declared that the future city would be everywhere and nowhere, and that it would be a city so greatly different from the ancient city or from any city today that we would probably fail to recognize its coming as a city at all. Elsewhere he stated, "America needs no help to Broadacre City, it will build itself haphazard." On the one hand Wright thought that one should consciously establish a new system of dispersed land-settlement throughout the country, while on the other, he thought that such an anti-metropolitan condition would come into being by itself. By the late 1920s, Wright had experienced the nascent deurbanization of America first-hand by habitually driving back and forth across the country between Wisconsin and Arizona. Thus, after condemning, at length, the dead and dying metropolis of rent and victimization, Wright turned to the impact of the mobilization and mass communication as brought about by the mass ownership of the automobile and by the concomitant convenience of modern telecommunications, including, all too prophetically, television. All this meant that the dense city of capital was no longer the essential instrument of technological and economic progress. For Wright in 1932, there were five agencies that were jointly responsible for bringing this about: (1) electrification; (2) the internal combustion engine independent of any form of fixed track; (3) electro-mechanical refrigerating and heating that could operate independent of the metropolis; (4) the existence of new lightweight materials that Wright saw as facilitating economic forms of low-density, residential land settlement; and (5) mechanized production in general, which since his 1901 lecture "The Art and Craft of the Machine" Wright had seen as the prime mover of a democratic, deurbanized American civilization.

At the same time, Wright acknowledged that none of this would achieve its fully liberative capacity without certain political changes—although he remained somewhat uncertain as to the exact nature of these. As with Ebenezer Howard, he thought Henry George's *Progress and Poverty* of 1879 held the key; although, like Howard, he had serious misgivings about the single tax theory. He was nonetheless positive about the promise of George's social vision:

> Democracy reintegrated as the systematized integration of small individual units built up high in the quality of individuality is a practical and rational ideal of freedom: machine in hand. Division of the exaggerated commercial-enterprise into more effective small units and reintegration over the whole surface of the nation—this is now no less practical. Communal ownership by way of taxation of all communal resources is not necessarily communism, as Henry George points out with complete logic. It may be entirely democratic.[4]

Later in *The Disappearing City* he would write about his automotive utopia in terms that, in retrospect, seem almost Futurist:

. . . spacious landscaped highways, grade crossings eliminated, "by-passing" living areas, devoid of the already archaic telegraph and telephone poles and wires and free of blaring billboards and obsolete construction. Imagine these great highways, bright with wayside flowers. . . Giant roads, themselves great architecture, pass public service stations, no longer eyesores, expanded to include all kinds of service and comfort.[5]

Wright was so enamored with this megalopolitan vision *avant la lettre*, that he was quite willing to accept automobile commutation of up to 150 miles one way as a normative standard. In this text, Wright already outlined many of the ideal building types of his Broadacre City model of 1932, including freestanding low-rise Usonian homes, tall freestanding towers for migrants and bachelors, silent, smokeless, small-scale factories, and resort hotels such as the one Wright projected for San Marcos in the desert. One of the key types in Broadacre City was the Walter Davidson model farm unit, exhibited at MoMA in 1940. Designed to facilitate the economic management of both home and land, the unit was critical to the economy of Broadacre, where every man would be allocated an acre of land at birth. Apart from George's economic theory, Wright patently based his ideal city on Peter Kropotkin's *Fields, Factories and Workshops* of 1899. Wright, like Henry Ford, refused to recognize the inherent contradiction of such a proposition, namely, that an individualistic, quasi-agrarian economy would not necessarily guarantee a regionally urbanized populace its subsistence or the benefits of Taylorized production, since the latter still demanded a certain concentration of both labor and resources. Kropotkin himself acknowledged the need to centralize the processes of heavy industry. Wright's vision of smallholders driving to rural factories in secondhand Model-T Fords suggests that a permanent, "sweaty equity" labor force would have been an essential aspect of the Broadacre economy.

Aside from continuing his diatribe against the hegemony of Hood and others—as in his *Architectural Forum* review of an Art Deco architectural show staged in Macy's department store—Wright encountered an entirely new protagonist in 1933, namely the Soviet Union, which, in the form of a wayward *Pravda* correspondent, first contacted him in the fall of that year [pages 74–75]. Wright was asked to comment on the fate of the American intellectual and state of intellectual life during the Depression, to which he responded:

No radical measures have been undertaken in the New Deal but there has been a great deal of tinkering and adjusting and pushing with prices to bring the old game alive again. Something more is needed than an arbitrary price system to re-awaken capitalistic confidence in the spending of money. . . It is now proposed among the more sensible of the intelligentsia that all absentee-ownership be declared illegal. . . In the course of the next five years a real demand for such "repeal" of special privilege may come to pass. This is the feeling of the minority among intelligentsia but they are doing nothing about it. They are spectators, by birth, breeding, and habit. Meantime all are getting on with about one-tenth of their former incomes.[6]

Seemingly dissatisfied with this, Wright wrote *Pravda* again soon after, arguing that the Depression had virtually eliminated the profession, which had in any event been previously reduced to the mere decoration of real estate, and that the entire capitalist system had done nothing but perpetuate a makeshift society. While praising the Soviet Union for its heroic attempt at a society based on human values, Wright nonetheless expressed his fear that it would degenerate into state capitalism and into a world solely dominated by Stakhanovite standards of Taylorized production. For him the issue was how to allow for individual creativity while still providing social justice for all.

Soon after this exchange, Wright received a further questionnaire from the magazine *Sovietskaya Architectura*, touching not only on sociopolitical issues but also on his working method. The questions ranged from technological constraints to conceptual development and from the role of drawing to the future place of the classical tradition in modern architectural production. These questions already reflected the imposition of Stalinist cultural policy and the emergence of a Socialist Realist party line in architecture as in the other arts. Wright's reply is one of the most concise and lucid statements of his career:

The solution of every problem is contained within itself. Its plan, form, and character are determined by the nature of the site, the nature of the materials used, the nature of the system using them, the nature of the life concerned, and the purpose of the building itself.[7]

Needless to say, while he was against any notion of composition in architecture or any kind of classical allusion, he often made use of classical composition in his own more extensive layouts. As to the role of drawing, he insisted that it was only a means to an end. Committed to the idea of the *Gesamtkunstwerk*, Wright thought that painting and sculpture should be fully integrated into the work, under the architect's control. He went on to stress the importance of site supervision and his general antipathy to last-minute refinements. He wrote: "Corrections, additions should be as few as possible. If sufficient study has been devoted to the development of the project they should be unnecessary."

When the "Century of Progress" exhibition opened in 1933, Wright denounced it yet again for being a miscarriage of modern architecture. Once more he laid the ultimate blame on the Exposition Internationale des Arts Décoratifs, which he saw, somewhat self-servingly, as an assimilation of his own Prairie manner and, more objectively, as a distortion of the organic architectural tradition of the Midwest. Feeling let down by his fellow architects and abandoned by the society, Wright wrote:

> The cause of an organic architecture as a living tradition is here betrayed just as the same old eclecticism has betrayed the dying Gothic tradition [a reference to Hood's Chicago Tribune Building of 1922] and as it has betrayed the dead pseudo-classic. It should not wholly betray the Renaissance because the Renaissance itself, where architecture was concerned, was a Roman holiday — a "Fair" — you may see the deeper and more profound work that is indigenous to their own country betrayed by way of its own countenance, used as a mask by the expedient eclecticism of unfair architects and sold as ballyhoo to the public in the name of "Progress."[8]

In the last analysis, Wright regarded the entire exhibition as a parody of his vision; as the proliferation of a pseudo-style similar to the White City classicism that, with the single exception of Louis Sullivan's Transportation Pavilion, had dominated the Chicago World's Columbian Exhibition of 1893. Even the colored floodlighting of the 1933 fair earned Wright's disapproval, for he saw it as a parody of Sullivan's polychromy.

In December 1933, Wright wrote the most "critical" version of the Taliesin Fellowship prospectus, wherein aside from claiming the manifest virtues of a hands-on apprenticeship system he also attacked the academic degeneracy of the professional architectural schools [page 76]. Needless to say it was also an advertisement for what the fellowship had achieved to date. Among many other achievements, both real and fictive, the reader is informed of the film archive that Wright had started to assemble in order to overcome the isolation of his Taliesin stronghold:

In the Taliesin Playhouse there has been and will be seen a series of five films projected by the excellent Western Electric sound equipment, films composed by such masters as Eisenstein, René Clair, Murnau, Chaplin, Disney, Pabst and other productions of fine character. The sound system is wired to speakers in other buildings of the group, in the living rooms and in the balcony of the central studio. Pianos are located in the studios and living room for apprentices to play. Facilities exist in the Playhouse for amateur theatricals. The Playhouse has a flexible stage, dressing rooms, rooms for designing and making sets and is adapted to concerts, lectures and fellowship gatherings as well as theater and cinema.[9]

Wright concluded the 1933 prospectus by discussing how all the other arts would be integrated into the culture of Taliesin, including painting, sculpture, and music. Following the Bauhaus's lead, he also envisaged a branching out into photography, printing, and publicity.

Throughout Wright's fallow period of the first half of the 1930s, when he had little work, he occupied himself at Taliesin by designing and fabricating a large demonstration model of Broadacre City that, ironically enough, was first exhibited in Hood's Rockefeller Center in 1934. At the same time he wrote a series of articles that, while going over old ground, as in his attack on the International Style and Le Corbusier, also opened up new themes, such as his "Two-Zone House," an article published in 1934 or his essay on architectural sculpture of 1935. In this last case, he revealed his longstanding admiration for the artists of the Viennese Secession: Klimt, Wagner, Hoffmann, and Olbrich. Written as a review of *The New Architectural Sculpture* by Walter Raymond Agard, this short notice began a series of reviews that he wrote at the time, including a generous appraisal of Paul Frankl's *Form and Reform: A Practical Handbook of Modern Interiors* and a more critical reading of Hugh Morrison's *Louis Sullivan: Prophet of Modern Architecture*. While Wright found in Frankl yet another native Viennese genius in the field of decorative art, he delivered a fresh account of the Adler and Sullivan partnership, in which he not only defended Sullivan against what he regarded as Morrison's misrepresentations, but also came to Adler's defense as Sullivan's functionalist teacher. With a display of misplaced loyalty rather than critical acumen, Wright repudiated Morrison's thesis that H. H. Richardson had exercised an influence on Sullivan. Finally, in a 1936 essay entitled "To the Memorial Craftsmen of America" [page 77], Wright condemned the American cult of venerating the dead through vertical tombstones and monuments. He advocated instead for the conversion of existing cemeteries into horizontally terraced parks, paved with commemorative marble slabs, very much like the cemetery that he designed for the Martin family in 1928, the so-called Blue Sky Burial Terraces.

As his "Two-Zone House" essay, published in the first issue of the lavish *Taliesin* magazine, indicates, Wright had by now evolved his concept of the fully modernized American home into a new plan type in which the kitchen was treated as a "work studio" partially open to the living space and the services condensed into a central core dividing the house into its quiet and active zones. Wright finally synthesized these ideas in his first Usonian L-plan courthouses of the mid-1930s, his Malcolm Willey House in Minneapolis of 1934, and his Herbert Jacobs House built in Madison, Wisconsin in 1936.

While Wright received two important commissions in 1936—the house Fallingwater for Edgar Kaufmann and the SC Johnson Administration Building—he was more aware than ever of the deepening economic depression and of the reconstruction policies then being pursued by Roosevelt's New Deal. In such a climate he became increasingly concerned that capitalism had reached an impasse and that only a fundamental change would enable the United States to restructure itself and to recover its former energy and direction. As to the political form that this change should take, Wright remained uncertain, except that it should conform to some kind of neo-capitalist social democracy, which accounted for his evident sympathy for the Netherlands and Scandinavia. This also explains the empathy he felt for the Soviet Union when he visited it with his wife, Olgivanna, in June 1937.

Despite the enforced collectivization and the purges of the Soviet elite, Wright felt that the Soviet Union was on the right track politically—or at least moving in a direction that would soon prove to be more effective than that of the United States. That Wright's view of all this was naive, not to say confused, is suggested by his breezy dismissal of the Trotskyite claim that the revolution was being betrayed. At the same time, Wright remained acutely aware that an equally radical change would have to be enacted in the United States if an organic modern society worthy of democracy was ever to be realized. In 1937, he wrote, "The Russian spirit in this new way of life over there, where 90 percent of the people are still what we call illiterate, is vigorous and healthy beyond any nation on earth. As I walked the streets among them I felt, God help any nation or nations either undertaking to interfere with this." Such enthusiasm, together with his categorical attack on land and money speculation as made in his address to the Chicago Real Estate Board in 1938, was sufficient to render him a radical suspect in the paranoid McCarthy era of the 1950s.

Notwithstanding his political sympathy, Wright dissociated himself from the pompier classicism of Stalinist Russia, seeing it as a betrayal of the revolution in architectural terms. In his 1937 *Izvestia* article he wrote [page 78]: "The buildings of a democracy will first know and love the nature of the ground upon which they stand. They will realize that the humble horizontal line is the line of human life upon this earth." At the same time, he understood only too well why the abstract, Constructivist architecture of the Soviet avant-garde should have been rejected by the Soviet state, for this once again was the international "neutered" functionalism against which he had been campaigning since the early 1930s. In a rather repetitious text of 1937, entitled *Architecture and Modern Life* [page 79], Wright, together with the philosopher Baker Brownell, attempted to further justify his radical proposals for reconstructing America. Hood's Radio City was again seen as symptomatic of all that was wrong with the vertical metropolis of New York as opposed to the low-rise horizontal city of Broadacre. The familiar diatribe aside, the most intriguing aspect of this book is the Socratic dialogue between Wright and Brownell, in which Brownell generally played Boswell to Wright's Johnson, although at times decidedly more astute.

In 1938, Wright was generally sympathetic to the achievements of the New Deal; and in an *Architectural Forum* [page 80] monograph on his work published in January, he itemized the nine essential precepts of the Usonian house as a general principle for future low-rise, low-cost, suburban development. Thus he advocated for the minimization of the roof, the provision of a carport, the elimination of the basement together with radiators and as much freestanding furniture as possible. As far as he was concerned, seating, like storage, should be built-in. This was Wright's "natural house" in the making, and as a result he came out against plastering, painting, gutters, and down pipes. By 1938, Wright could set forth his modernized organic architecture as a total program from the smallest prefabricated house to a total deurbanization strategy as the ultimate model for future development. This was the message that he took to England when he was invited to give the George Watson lectures at the Royal Institute of British Architects (RIBA) in London in April 1939. Appropriately enthusiastic, this volume concludes with the edited transcript of the four lectures, published in England in that year under the title *An Organic Architecture: The Architecture of Democracy* [page 81]. Wright rose to the royal occasion of his appearance at the RIBA by making an iridescent presentation of his life's work, complete with films of Taliesin West under construction. While covering the familiar Broadacre argument, he pointedly referred to a categoric stand against commodity speculation and usury. This messianic stance brought about an intelligent and sometimes aggressive response that Wright mostly managed to field with wit and sagacity. However, when once pushed into a corner, he was forced to concede that he did not recommend dismantling the historic urban centers of the world where they existed and were justly revered.

Shortly after the lectures were published, the whole of Europe was at war for the second time in twenty years. One year later, in 1940, when he was seventy-three, Wright was honored in absentia with the Gold Medal of the Royal Institute of British Architects, the eighth in the line of such similar honors, as he wryly remarked in the postwar edition of his autobiography.

Notes

1. Frank Lloyd Wright, "Of Thee I Sing," *Shelter* 2 (April 1932); reprinted in Bruce Brooks Pfieffer, ed., *Frank Lloyd Wright: Collected Writings*, vol. 3 (New York: Rizzoli, 1992), 113–115.

2. Frank Lloyd Wright, "Why We Want This School," in *The Hillside Home School of the Allied Arts* (Spring Green, WI: Frank Lloyd Wright, 1931), 1; item 2401.056, version A, The Frank Lloyd Wright Foundation Archives (The Museum of Modern Art | Avery Architectural and Fine Arts Library, Columbia University, New York).

3. Wright, "What Would the School Produce," in *The Hillside Home School of the Allied Arts*.

4. Frank Lloyd Wright, *The Disappearing City* (New York: William Farquhar Payson, 1932), 33.

5. Wright, *The Disappearing City*, 44.

6. Frank Lloyd Wright letter to Moissaye J. Olgin, October 26, 1933, item 2401.135, version F, The Frank Lloyd Wright Foundation Archives.

7. Frank Lloyd Wright, "Categorical Reply to Questions by Architecture of the USSR," December 7, 1933, item 2401.136, version B, The Frank Lloyd Wright Foundation Archives.

8. Frank Lloyd Wright, "The Chicago World's Fair," *The Architect's Journal*, vol. 78 (July 1933): 45–47; reprinted in Pfieffer, *Frank Lloyd Wright: Collected Writings*, vol. 3, 155.

9. Frank Lloyd Wright, "Integration," in *The Taliesin Fellowship* (Spring Green, WI: Frank Lloyd Wright, 1933), 2.

THE HILLSIDE HOME SCHOOL OF THE ALLIED ARTS.

Why We Want This School

AMERICA has provided innumerable schools, academic, vocational or free in which to educate its children. Americans are proud of the results with good reason. America, too, has trade-schools and a few industrial schools of a more or less formal or sentimental pattern.

A minority report is needed at this psychological moment. It seems high time to plan for the super-structure we are to rear upon the elaborate educational preparations we have so expensively and laboriously made, from Kindergarten to University, for a past century or more.

We have no super-structure, that is to say no culture above the matters of behaviour, commerce, industry, politics and an unsure taste for objects d'art. It may even appear that the preparation or foundation was inadequate and in the wrong place.

We are a nation rich beyond the bounds, even of our own avarice, living in abundance with a creature-comfort undreamed of in the World before. We are ingenious, inventive, scientifically, commercially progressive and, as the whole World has occasion to know — uncreative.

We have had many sympathetic critics, some of them worthy of attention, who repeatedly and pointedly call our attention to this fact.

Nor will more than three-fifths of our people know what is meant by the assertion that the American is "uncreative." Another fifth would deny the allegation pointing to our magnificent machinery and scientific accomplishments to refute the charge.

About one man in a hundred would agree with the stricture and admit it. But he would apologize on the ground that we are a pioneering people, with a continent to make habitable and workable, while as a Nation we are digesting not the best elements of the Nationalities of the World.

Like the Chicago Captain of Industry at the dinner given C. R. Ashbee, famous London Arts and Craftsman and architect, when Ashbee arrived in Chicago some fifteen years ago and criticized the City for its ugliness.

The Captain sat it out as long as he could, then got his feet under him to say that: "Ashbee may be right, Chicago isn't much on Culture now . . . maybe. But when Chicago gets after Culture, she'll make Culture hum."

—1—

"Why We Want This School," in *The Hillside Home School of the Allied Arts,* written in 1931 after the closing of the original Hillside Home School in Spring Green, Wisconsin, designed by Wright and founded by his aunts in 1886. Inspired by the "learn by doing" educational model of the school, Wright and his wife Olgivanna decided to reopen the Hillside Home School buildings as an institution for architecture and allied arts. It was later integrated it into the Taliesin Fellowship.

OF THEE I SING

Architecture is our blind spot. Of course
our people did get here from abroad. So no wonder we have
had no architecture of our own except what we-the-people" had
on when we came over. We got ours that way and can be sold the
wrong kind now from the same source.

But we have been on our own, a civilization
professing Democracy (and practicing nearly everything else)
for a long time now. Since 1776 to be exact and yet our ignorance
as to what constitutes an appropriate significant building
here in our own country is becoming a serious deficit, one to
be shaken up, understood and settled before we will ever be
a culture we can honestly call our own. One not hopelessly
mongrel or basely subservient.

A witty Frenchman said "we are [OF US] the only great
nation to proceed [HATE] [ED] directly from barbarism to degeneracy with
no culture of our [ITS] own in between".

We do seem in danger of being not only bastard but,
now, of looking like a dummy in a show window [ALL GLASS CAGE] accepting a European
cliché for an architecture instead of realizing that we have ONE OF OUR OWN [ALREADY]
A BETTER ONE already evolved out of our own life on our own soil; an ideal
democratic way of building, [A WAY OF BUILDING] which our people might now recognize
as our own and love for what it really is: not only a valid
expression of the spirit of Liberty but most appropriate to
our own way of being somebody in our own right, by Being ourselves.

"Of Thee I Sing" was originally published in *Shelter* magazine (April 1932). Wright continued working on the theme, and the version shown here is a typescript dated July 24, 1953.

THE DISAPPEARING CITY

The Disappearing City, published by W. F. Payson in New York, 1932. The book was considered the theoretical elaboration of the Broadacre City model first exhibited in Rockefeller Center, New York in 1934.

ПРАВДА

«Pravda» Moscow

Moissaye J. Olgin
American Correspondent
35 E. 12th Street, New York
ALgonquin 4-9481

October 19, 1933

Mr. Frank Lloyd Wright
Taliesen Spring
Green, Wis.

Dear Mr. Wright:

A year ago the Pravda asked your opinion about
the position of the intellectuals in the United States
in connection with the economic crisis. Your opinion
was then forwarded to Moscow. Today the Pravda editors
wishing to acquaint their readers more thoroughly with
the changes wrought in the life of the intellectuals
during the last year, solicit your opinion on the following questions:

ПРАВДА

«Pravda» Moscow

Moissaye J. Olgin
American Correspondent
35 E. 12th Street, New York
ALgonquin 4-9481

1. What change, if any, has taken place in the life
of the intellectuals (engineers, technicians, architects,
artists, writers, teachers, etc.)during the last year?

2. How has the prolongation of the crisis influenced the creative activities in this country in the
realm of technique, art, literature and the sciences?

3. Do you see improvement ahead for the intellectual groups?

An early reply will be highly appreciated.

Yours sincerely,

Moissay J Olgin

Letter to Wright from Moissaye J. Olgin, the American correspondent to the
Moscow newspaper *Pravda*, October 19, 1933, inquiring about the state of
intellectual life in the US.

My dear Mr. Olgin:

Little visible change in the life or the attitude toward life of the intelligentzia of the United States is evident. No clear thinking is possible to them. They are all the hapless beneficiaries of a success-system they have never clearly understood, but a system that worked miracles for them while they slept. The hardships of the last three years have left them confused but not without hope that more miracles will come to pass in their behalf. They are willing to wait for them to happen.

The Capitalistic system is a gambling game. It is hard to cure gamblers of gambling and everybody high and low in this country prefers the gamblers chance at a great fortune to the slower growth of a more personal fortune.

It is true that the educational system of the country has for many decades been breeding inertia. It aims to produce the middle class mind which is able to function only in the middle of the road, boulevard preferred. It is the "safe" mind for thee system as set up.

Machine-power is vicarious power at best and breeds a lower type of individuality, it seems, the longer it functions. Action of any sort becomes less and less likely. So Creative activity is a thing of the past— so far as it goes with machinepowersqin these United States. Little art of any but the most superficial lind— the formula or the fashion— now characterizes the life of the States. The capacity for spiritual rebellion has grown small and the present ideals of success are making it smaller every day. No radical measures have been undertaken in the New Deal but there has been a great deal of tinkering and adjusting and pushing with

Wright's letter back to Olgin, October 26, 1933. Of the US intelligentsia, Wright wrote: "They are all hapless beneficiaries of a success-system they have never clearly understood, but a system that worked miracles for them while they slept."

76   *The Taliesin Fellowship*, published by The Taliesin Press in Spring Green, Wisconsin, 1933.

To the Memorial Craftsmen of America

PALMER HOUSE
CHICAGO

I am glad you sent for —

Concerning this business of dying and leaving to leave "one of those things" — You, memorial craftsmen of America, are chiefly occupied in distinguishing or making distinguished the houses of the dead — whereas the architect is busy — if he is busy — making distinguished the houses of the quick; so quick to distinguish the houses of the quick, alive not so quick some dead or thirty awaiting burial at sixty —

I think it timely on your part because — after all is said and done, there in hamlets, villages and cities of the dead your work adorns are not ready for the dead but for the living quick to the living, the hamlets towns and cities my work attempts to make for one habitable are for the living. I think therefore these places we call cemetery should be more pleasurable habitations for the dead — less dead to the living — to the living as less so?

Let's talk it over — a habitation for the living is placed First the sense by the realtor and "the lot" is only sensible whereas an acre of ground was never before American minimum now if it is just the cemetery for the dead majesty the realtor by two alive and gets another as long as he is tall and as wide as he is long when he moves down and out or more correct lies up and down — there is no sense in this realtor's curse in either case — And I believe if the resting places of the quick and the dead are to be made more beautiful — ground must be more sensibly and generously used for that purpose, the matter begins right there and there is nothing to do until the realtors are wounded up, taken out, to be shot at sunrise.

"To The Memorial Craftsmen of America," written on Palmer House stationery, November 1936.

FOR "IZVESTIA"

Here is to you, Democratic Russia, the interior nature of man working
its way into a naturally beautiful way of life, hoping you will soon see
architectural forms of hereditary aristocracy as just as false to any
naturally beautiful way of life as the old aristocracy itself was false to
human rights.

Facism, the resort of nations in weakness or despair, may accept the
old forms with modern improvements, because Facism is merely man attempting to
work out a pattern of life and impose it upon men from the outside.
Nations which have lived under capitalism or aristocracy too long become
senile and bewildered and helplessly accept the dictator. But Facism
cannot know Principle. It only knows the approved fashion.

Russian Democracy that shed its blood to reject the aristocratic wrong
only to spend its best energies in continuing the false forms of that
aristocracy where culture is concerned—as it is being continued in architecture
and the arts in Soviet Russia today, must not be too patient with that
cultural-lag. The cultural forms of the old regime were betrayals of their
originals and can only betray your new reality. They will make of your
priceless youth a premature reality.

Capitalism too, helplessly accepts the false forms of hereditary aristocracy and applies them to whatever is new. Nothing is more capitalistic than
the skyscraper and its elevator. With capitalism as with Facism, the auto-
cratic Beaux Arts sits in the shadow of government as a cultural lag to render
cultural acts null and void—shirking reality as irksome if not vulgar.

"For Izvestia," written for the Russian newspaper's twentieth-anniversary issue
on "culture under facism and culture in the USSR," 1937.

ARCHITECTURE AND MODERN LIFE

BY BAKER BROWNELL AND
FRANK LLOYD WRIGHT

ILLUSTRATED

HARPER & BROTHERS PUBLISHERS
NEW YORK AND LONDON MCMXXXVII

THE ARCHITECTURAL FORUM • JANUARY 1938

To take this matter of an organic architecture
a little deeper into the place where it belongs—
the human heart—the design matter in this issue falls readily into the following sensuous expressions of principle at work. It is a sense of the
whole that is lacking in the "modern" buildings
I have seen, and we are here concerned with that
sense of the whole which alone is radical.

1. The sense of the ground. (Topography, organic features. Growth.)
2. The sense of shelter.
3. The sense of materials. (Illustrated by characteristic early plans—showing interior living
space becoming exterior architecture. Character-
istic plans—early and late—abolishing walls,
interior partitions, etc., and grouping or placing
utilitarian features in such manner as to allow
space to be either magnified or uninterrupted so

for as possible.)
4. The sense of space.
5. The sense of proportion. (With this you must
be born. An instinct.)
6. The sense of order. (Related by cultivation to
the sense of proportion.)
7. Ways and means, that is to say, technique.
Last and least. Each man his own.

Characterizing these expressions in various
forms—each an actual experience—plot-plans,
plans, perspectives and photographs, some re-
minders of early buildings alongside later buildings. I have always considered plans most essential in the presentation or consideration of
any building. There is more beauty in a fine
ground plan itself than in almost any of its consequences. So plot-plans and structural plans
have been given due place in this issue as of first
importance. Furniture and planting are indicated

on them. Next,—the perspective study of the
original concept. Then, photographs of finished
structures and those in course of construction.
Finally—certain details of these Usonian* buildings.

*Usonia was Samuel Butler's name for these United States.

CONTENTS . . . JANUARY 1938

80

Table of contents drafted by Wright for a special Wright-themed issue
of *Architectural Forum*, vol. 68, no. 1 (January 1938).

Speaking strictly these spontaneous talks were not intended to be "lectures" on Architecture.

Had I been commissioned to give them by the Royal Institute of British Architects instead of the Sulgrave Manor Board they might have been, properly, so limited.

But it seemed to me more appropriate upon this occasion to consider the place Architecture must have in Society if Democracy is to be realized.

An Organic Architecture means more or less organic society. Organic ideals of integral building reject rules imposed by exterior æstheticism or mere taste, and so would the people to whom such architecture would belong reject such external impositions upon life as were not in accord with the nature and character of the man who had found his work and the place where he could be happy and useful because of it in some scheme of livelihood fair to him.

Where there is no general scheme of livelihood fair and square with him, and wide open to his development as a better man, I do not see much hope for good architecture.

From Usonia to Asia Minor—poking about among the ruins of cultures mankind has known—anyone may see how the one quarrelled with the next and like dogs all ate one another up as they could.

All, ruined, lie tumbled or crumbled together, the few grains of sense possessed by each all coming to the same thing in the end. No ideal seems to have had power enough or beauty to *resist* the fateful law of change in any of its many manifestations. Institution followed by Destitution is the common sequence.

Beauty seems to have made no sense long at any time. I believe the time has come when Beauty must make sense for our time at least. And as man emerges, by way of ages of experience, upon the scene of these fateful tragedies precipitated upon himself by his own æsthetic when divorced from his own common sense, the falsity, therefore the impotence of his education, generation by generation, becomes a little clearer to him.

Youth is with me, I believe, in this youthful faith. This faith will be the gist of these talks for four evenings from the Sir George Watson Chair in this great room of the Royal Institute of British Architects . . . walls lined with young British architects.

I find it safer to try to build it than to try to "say it" because in construction sophistry falls down whereas tactful language has the disconcerting knack of outliving itself.

Another thing I should mention: in going about on the vast, varied surfaces of mother Earth I have seen that, whenever and wherever man builded best and his common sense *did* make beauty and beauty made sense, then and there only are buildings to be found made by the people out of the ground in ways of their own devising—true to time, place, environment and purpose. Folk building we might call them.

Folk-song grew into great symphony, but for 500 years wherever the "academic" entered building

An Organic Architecture: The Architecture of Democracy, published by Lund Humphries in London, 1939. In the forward to the book, Wright admitted: "I find it safer to try to build than to try to 'say it' because in construction sophistry falls down whereas tactful language has the disconcerting knack of outliving itself."

1939–1949

Wright's essays written between 1939 and 1949 carry forward many of the themes that he had broached in the 1930s, above all the unremitting attacks on all his familiar aversions: his ambivalence toward the state, his antipathy for the monumental "grandomania" of the École des Beaux-Arts, now extended to its successor, the Art Deco movement, and his repudiation of contemporary architecture at its most abstract — the so-called reductive functionalism of the International Style that for Wright certainly included Russian Constructivism.

The early 1940s, however, introduced a new target, namely the inevitable involvement of America in yet another world war. In retrospect, it seems that this pending conflict traumatized him to such a degree that he felt compelled to reassert his categorical opposition to all war, along with the eccentricity of his own political position. Thus we find him writing, as early as November 1940, in an essay entitled "Wake Up America!" [page 97], the following inflammatory declaration:

> During several months past I could "listen in" or read at any time anywhere and imagine myself back in the stupid days of 1914. But that previous catastrophe to the economy and morale of our democratic world was nothing compared to what now takes us in its grip. Shame enough to sell out our best thought at first sign of danger and see our nationals run pell-mell to play a second-hand imitation of the enemy when our power

can never lie in saving empire unless we too are empirical. Imitation is always base, and never yet won a battle. No, our real enemy is not Hitler! Our real enemy lies in our own timidity and stupidity as seen in this frightful current so smoothly moved, coaxed in the direction of self-destruction. "To save Britain?" No, to maintain Britain as our only shield against our own slavery or destruction is the insane notion sold to mediocrity by way of its own salesmen, from chief executive to the journalistic horde.[1]

Although this, in many respects, was only an extension of the pacifism that he had already expressed during the 1914–1918 conflict, there is a discernible, if subtle, allusion to his partiality for Teutonic culture, to such a degree that whereas he scrupulously disowned fascism as such, he nonetheless viewed the Third Reich as a distant, economic threat rather than as a totalitarian power bent on world domination. Moreover, he indulged elsewhere in sentiments touched by antisemitism:

But, if as a people we are going on to ultimate victory over selfish or vengeful interests that infect us because those interests are unable to feel outside their own pockets, see beyond their own factory floors, or rise about their murdered European relatives, it will go on alive only because the country can see with the help of its own free minority the murderous character of "power-politics" as played in unison by the two parties and realize the utter folly of such make-shift money-getting as is now in action. Why do our people not realize that it is this make-shift money-system that is the real danger now? That system is there at the bottom of this cry "save Britain." The system knows it well. Mass mediocrity does not know it.[2]

Elsewhere, after Pearl Harbor, he expressed a certain sympathy for Japanese imperial claims—electing to see this as a natural fulfillment of the Orient's desire to establish an imperium of its own.

Needless to say such views led him into conflict with many of his colleagues, including his faithful friend Lewis Mumford, who eventually lost his only son in the war, and his cousin Richard Lloyd Jones, newspaper editor and blockhouse client, who, according to Wright, told him: "Hell, Frank, if you don't like the system on which this country's run, why don't you get out of it? Go somewhere else! God-dammit." Later, Wright even fell foul of the infamous Senator McCarthy from Wisconsin, who in the full flood of his demagogic career attempted to have Wright impeached as an anti-American communist.

To characterize Wright's attitude at this time as isolationism is to miss the complexity of his vision—above all his persistent evocation of what was surely an unprecedented form of capitalism, if it was capitalism at all. This was a hypothetically restructured economy that he characterized as economic nationalism—the ramifications of which were surely as revolutionary as anything envisaged by Karl Marx, for whom Wright professed a marked distaste, if not total disdain. While professing after Ralph Waldo Emerson that the best form of government was the one that intervened the least, Wright nonetheless conjured up a utopia in which all useful inventions would at once enter the public domain, with the inventor being appropriately compensated by the state. An equally egalitarian provision would be to reserve for each citizen a certain quantum of interest-free national credit—a scheme patently modeled after C. H. Douglas's *Social Credit*, first published in 1924. Thus, as Wright put it, the state would assure that "neither land nor money nor creative ideas can be speculative commodities to be traded or held over by somebody against the common good." Hence the equally zany notion, as set forth in *The Disappearing City* (1932), of reserving an acre of land for every American at birth. In 1941, a year after "Wake Up America!," in an article devoted to the work of G. Hickling, the editor of the English magazine *Reality*, Wright followed Hickling's views by arguing that since America was self-sufficient she could pioneer the Social Credit system with impunity—she could feed her population and remain solvent irrespective of whether she had an excess of imports or exports.

Hickling was not the only British Social Credit theorist to whom Wright turned in these years, as one may judge from Stanley C. Norton, who contributed an important short essay on economic theory to the second volume of the *Taliesin* magazine. The essay was devoted to elaborating on the economic implications of that which Norton called "The New Frontier:"

> The idea of the new system lies in a form of true "Economic Nationalism"—putting our own house in order first, making one's own country sound economically and financially. Briefly, instead of the issue of money and credit being the monopoly of private financier-money-lenders, it will become the function of the state. Credit will be socialized. Money will become a medium of exchange, of distribution, and not a commodity in the hands of private firms to be let out on hire. The government will

create money for defense and for all public works and social services; this money being backed by the credit of the country, as is the case when government borrows from private banks, but it would be free of interest and it would not come out of the taxpayer's pockets. A form of National Dividend will replace relief and all social-security payments. The controlled "Just Price," which will replace the present prices swollen by overheads and selling costs, will be instituted for all necessities. In place of the exchange of goods for gold, or gold for gadgets, there will be among the countries an exchange of needed goods for needed goods.[3]

However naive and utopian this economic theory of need may have been, it was echoed by Wright, in what presumably was his own critique of American plutocratic capitalism. Like Le Corbusier, he was categorically opposed to the emergence of modern consumerism as a form of engineered wastage on a mammoth scale.

Thus we cannot judge Wright's pacifist tracts of the early 1940s—he wrote ten such essays between 1940 and 1942—without setting them against the frustration and anger he felt with regard to the fundamentally wasteful character of American civilization, particularly given the disaster of the Great Depression that, notwithstanding Roosevelt's New Deal, had such a devastating effect not only on the country as a whole but also on his own practice. The full dimension of the burden that this imposed upon the sixty-five-year-old Wright, as he attempted to both rebuild his aunts' Hillside Home School and to initiate the Taliesin Fellowship, is compellingly set forth in Book Five of the second edition of *An Autobiography* [page 96] published in 1943 under the section subtitled "Form:"

We needed, and desperately, lumber, stone, lime, and laborers of all sorts. As you see in the lines (and between them), we had very little or no money at all to pay for these coveted desirables... We were now where we had to have more lumber or stop work altogether. Standing around in the woods of our country, were many piles of sawed oak. I coveted them all as I coveted gravel, sand, and cement... I tried to buy some of these lumber piles, pay part down, part on credit. But nothing could be done. The hard financial situation all around had made everyone, especially the farmers, doubly suspicious, especially so of me, the spender of so much money with no visible means of support... I drove over to see Herb, offered him a fair price and terms for four hundred acres of timber, on the stump... Then I found a good sawer on the other side of the river who agreed to saw the logs at the regular price if we cut them and brought them in... Forthwith, we went headlong into logging. The place became a logging camp. Soon, after overcoming innumerable difficulties of a time-consuming, painful but picturesque character, green-oak timber was going up into the walls and trusses of our coveted buildings... But we had to have lime or stop... The lumberyards were full of cement — but for us to keep our work going, deliveries were only for cash-down. The cement dealers, like the lumber dealers, all knew the way out of the scrape they were in: stick together. Keep prices up... Strictly up against it again, under pressure, I remembered that the lime for the original Hillside Home School buildings... had all been burned in the hills not more than several miles away. The old kiln might be there yet! ... So up went the boys to bring the old wrecked lime-kiln back to life again and themselves learn how to burn lime: a bunch of greensters. I got an old-time lime-burner from Black Earth to instruct them. We fixed up the broken gates with old ones we took from the old buildings at Hillside — patched up the tumbled walls, stripped a section of the old stone quarry and filled the patched-up restoration with good raw lime rock; piled cords and cords of wood alongside in long ranks to feed the roaring fires... We got good lime... hundreds of bushels of it. We could have gone into the lime business, and thought seriously of doing so... There was no building. Little money was coming in to go into so many hands, and without any, some of the men began to get ugly. But they would go away with a little. During many ensuing weeks there were outrageous scenes. One, Jones, a troublesome ringleader, attacked me in the studio one late afternoon — got his hands well on towards my throat when Henry jumped at him, yelling so loud with anger that Jones was scared "into taking his hands off Mr. Wright."[4]

It was with such telling anecdotes as these, rather anachronically arranged, that Wright patched together this fifth book. In the revised version of *An Autobiography*, Wright elected to subdivide the original Book One into two books, dealing with fellowship and family separately, thereby transforming Book Two and Book Three into the third and fourth book respectively, and summarily adding "Form" before going to press. A sixth book was prepared to add relatively minor details to the original account of the Broadacre concept — but was presumably never included because it was seen as rather superfluous to information already set forth in *The Disappearing City* (1932), which was later reworked in 1945 in *When Democracy Builds* [page 107]. This was in turn revised again in 1958 in the book *The Living City*, just one year before his death. What is not repeated here, nor anywhere else for that matter, is Wright's wholly ambivalent attitude toward state control; for although he remained opposed to bureaucracy in all its forms, and above all to building codes, he nonetheless thought that government should intervene when it came to the provision of basic infrastructure, particularly with regard to the conservation of his beloved Arizona desert and the panoramic site of his own Taliesin West. Even more specifically, Wright wanted the government to protect him from the US Army Corps of Engineers who, notwithstanding his petitioning the president, still persisted in installing power lines across the desert panorama of Taliesin West.

Despite his belief in the manifest destiny of the democratic state, Wright clearly felt that the present federation of the United States was too cumbersome and that the nation should be subdivided along regional and cultural lines into the three separate states: Usonia, Usonia South, and New England. This is set forth in an essay of that title written in 1941 [page 99]:

> If this union, now divided into forty-eight separate states, is ever to be freed from equivocal British domination. . . it would be far better, and much the lesser of all probable evils to rearrange the states into a more simple and characteristic federation, a grouping of all the states into three principal states. Allow New England to keep the national capital and the official buildings of the present city of Washington as a present from the greater part of the nation.
>
> There is now pressing upon us the need for a far greater national capital. . . probably placed midway on the rolling prairies of the great Mid-West beside the Father of Waters—our Mississippi: there where the amplitude, rectitude and impartiality that might characterize the greater part of our nation, could, unhampered by congenital prejudice or the equivocal influence of foreign powers, be free to initiate and grow the ways and means to live a good life as the independent democracy this country was designed to be. . . According to geography, climate, natural self-interest and sentiment, three general state-groupings are manifest. They are the New England states, the Southern states including Texas and the great intermediate body of the Union. . . Were such equitable and better-fitting boundaries established in our country and this more simple and democratic system of election, one more directly responsible to the people, set up: my Lords, Ladies and Gentlemen I give you USONIA, USONIA SOUTH AND NEW ENGLAND: THE UNITED STATES OF AMERICA.[5]

With so many essays and books treating the same themes, repetition is unavoidable, and one often finds oneself wading through a great deal of reiterative material to get at the kernel of Wright's thought, which, once encountered, seems even now to be surprisingly fresh and insightful. That Wright needed much closer editing than Olgivanna or Eugene Masselink or anyone could provide goes without saying. As the essay "Form" reveals, Wright was certainly not above mocking his editors by persisting with his romantic rhetoric in the face of their critical commentary.

These essays reveal only too clearly how Wright's anti-interventionist stance of the early 1940s was intimately bound up with his broader political views and how these in turn were inextricable from the socioeconomic and technical implications of his Broadacre City thesis, the full elaboration of which was first made available to *Taliesin* subscribers in 1941 in part as a series of negative slogans [page 98]. Thus one learned in short order that Broadacre City was dead-set against officialdom, policemen, slums, landlords, and suspended power or communication lines, which were not permitted on the surface. By a similar token, regarding utilities, Wright insisted that coal should not be burnt except at the source. Hence Broadacre City projected a smokeless form of regional urbanization exclusively fed by automobiles and electrically powered monorails, with trains running at speeds of up to 200 mph. To these recommendations were added the recycling of sewage as fertilizer and the introduction of concave, floodlit roadbeds without ditches so that the stormwater would be conducted to a central grated gulley that would also serve as a dividing strip.

In that same year, in an essay entitled "Defense" [page 106], Wright posited a further list of undesirable practices that were advanced as the sociopolitical corollaries, so to speak, of his deurbanization thesis. Among the barbaric sentiments and pursuits of the Western world that Wright would have liked to see proscribed, one may note militarism (and with it conscription), patriotism, imperialism, academicism, journalism, fashion, organized sport, and mass entertainment of all kinds—from Broadway to Hollywood. Parts of this critique read like passages from Simone Weil's *The Need for Roots* of 1943, in which she made similar arguments. She posited above all that one cannot expect ordinary people to sacrifice their lives for a homeland in which they have no ultimate stake.

Of all Wright's anti-interventionist essays, the most prophetic by far was his 1941 *Taliesin Square-Paper* piece "Of What Use Is a Great Navy with No Place to Hide?" [pages 100–103], an essay that all too uncannily foresaw the Japanese destruction of the American fleet at Pearl Harbor on December 7, 1941. In the essay "Good Afternoon, Editor Evjue" [pages 104–105], published in Madison, Wisconsin's *The Capital Times*, on May 19, 1941, Wright even anticipated Roosevelt's strategy of provocation—that is, his deliberate massing of the fleet as a sitting target.

Throughout these writings of the early 1940s, together with the fifth book in his autobiography, a number of dyadic polarities are constantly alluded to. Wright insisted on the indisputable virtues of a mixed economy with the emphasis falling, as always, on the agrarian, on "tillage" as he liked to call it, as the key to self-sufficiency. Aside from this particular antinomy, there is sufficient evidence that Wright saw the world as a series of irreconcilable antagonisms. Thus he opposed nature to history, culture to education, apprenticeship to scholarship, salesmanship to statesmanship, and, last but not least, experiment to experimental. In a similar vein, he saw the master builder as one capable of conceiving of everything from the landscape to the interior, as opposed to the professional architect, who in Wright's view was only capable of designing grandiloquent shells. At the same time, deurbanization was the overriding credo that reappeared constantly in his writings from the early 1930s on; although, on his official visit to the Soviet Union in 1937 he seemed to have been totally oblivious to the fact that the Russian avant-garde had been preoccupied with a very similar issue. While Wright was deprecating about the then-official plan for the expansion of Moscow, he was surprisingly charitable to the young architects of the Soviet state, including Boris Iofan, who despite the "grandomania" of his winning design for the Palace of the Soviets was in Wright's good graces for his streamlined USSR Pavilion, built for the Paris World Exposition of 1937.

Soon after receiving the Guggenheim Museum commission from Hilla Rebay in 1943, Wright encountered yet another antagonist with whom he tussled for the hearts and minds of the world's most democratic state, namely the already infamous New York Commissioner Robert Moses, whose technocratic approach to planning the New York region did not sit well with Wright. Needless to say, Wright's Broadacre City thesis did not find much sympathy from the bureaucracy of Moses's Triborough Bridge Authority. Antithetical to housing as any kind of solution to the social and environmental problems confronting the modern city, Wright had the temerity to be critical of Moses's high-rise, high-density housing proposals, while Moses lost no time cutting Wright down to size:

> While we were generally familiar with your publications and views, my
> little group of earnest thinkers, or rather constructors, have read the

Taliesin Pamphlet and your more recent memorandum with considerable interest. The consensus of opinion is that we do not fully understand them. Some of the implications are most interesting, and, of course, we respect your accomplishments in the field of architecture, but it seems to us you have taken on a little too much territory. Most of my boys would feel you would get further if you tried an experiment on a reasonable scale, frankly called it an experiment and refrained from announcing that it was the pattern of all future American living.[6]

As it turned out, the Moses administration remained fairly hostile to Wright even as an architect, as one could judge from their sporadic but continual opposition to the realization of the Guggenheim (which would have never seen the light of day had it not been for Rebay's persistence and Wright's determination, not to mention the decision in 1957 by Harry Guggenheim, after Solomon R. Guggenheim's death in 1949, to put the Guggenheim fortune fully behind erecting the building). Be this as it may, Wright was already locking horns with Moses over the building a decade before. In his 1947 essay "Prejudice, Sir, Is a Disease" [page 108], Wright explained:

> I suggest that Robert Moses (the man) actually see the model of the new museum designed as a great gift from a great New Yorker to his own great city for a purpose. As an individual or an official Moses owed this to himself before, "carte blanche," he generalized so freely concerning this great thing which he reads about in the paper or only hears about from the boys in his backroom where there is ample reason to believe they are blind to the world-wide trend which they choose to see as "functionalism."[7]

Despite Wright's lifelong ambivalence toward the university, he had sufficient cause to be grateful to the generic institution: first, for sustaining him at a difficult moment in his career, to wit the Kahn lectures he gave at Princeton University in 1930; second, for the invitation he received in 1946 from his hometown university to participate in a seminar dedicated to "Works of the Mind." For all that he prided himself on always speaking spontaneously without notes, he seemed to have taken such formal presentations seriously, rising to this particular occasion with a well-crafted piece. However, with this particular address, at the University of Chicago under the title "The Architect," Wright was as perceptive and audacious on the subject of human creativity as anything from the pen of the French mathematician Henri Poincaré, only now from a predictably different standpoint:

> As for my share in this discussion (or presentation) of various phases of human activity, said to proceed from the mind, it is my belief that for five hundred years at least we have had no architecture which did proceed from the Mind.
>
> So here at the beginning we might as well clear up a little ambiguity concerning what we are in the habit of calling the Mind. Some of us laughingly (and wrongly) refer to our "minds." But the Mind should be not only a matter of the head (the intellect) but an affair of the heart and of the imagination and of the hand (or what we call technique). . . As I have said, we mistake memory, association of ideas, rationalizations, ratiocination—we mistake all that hypnosis and hallucination for thinking. But none of it is thinking at all. Do you realize that a great musician, if he is a performer, does not really have to think? Very few professors ever have to think. A mathematician does not have to think. You can study mathematics all your life and never do a bit of thinking. . . Thinking is an intense concentration of which few people are capable or even aware. It is a going-within, somehow, penetrating into the very nature of some objective: going in after gaining adequate experience of nature. . . and *staying in* there until you get what you went in after. You may not get it the first time, and you may not get it the second. And you may spend half your life trying to get into that place where the thing you are seeking really is—where it lives—finally to find the plane upon which what we call Reality really lives. But once you do find it—what a reward![8]

A comparable charm and wit was present in his 1949 AIA Gold Medal acceptance address [page 109], only this time it was combined with an exceptional openness and warmth, all the more surprising and touching given Wright's lifelong hostility to the profession and his arrogant habit of expressing nothing but contempt for most of his colleagues. Above all, one is struck by his magnanimity in graciously accepting belated recognition from his peers, exactly a decade after the British had accorded him the RIBA Gold Medal in 1939:

> No man climbs so high or sinks so low that he isn't eager to receive the good will and admiration of his fellow man. He may be reprehensible in many ways; he may seem to care nothing about it; he may hitch his wagon

to his star, but however he may be circumstanced or whatever his ideals or his actions, he never loses desire for the approbation of his kind.

So I feel humble and grateful.
Upon this really fine occasion of our presence here I don't think
    humility a very becoming state for me.
But I really feel deeply touched by this token of esteem from the
    home boys.
Honors have reached me from almost every great nation of
    the world.
Honor has, however, been a long time coming from home.
But here it is at least. Handsomely indeed.
Yes. . . I am extremely grateful.[9]

Wright did not leave it there, however, and those who were lulled into thinking they might only have to endure an entertaining and somewhat outrageous speech were led by degrees into a challenging—not to say extremely somber—discourse. Halfway through his address, the audience was forcibly brought to ponder the fate of architecture in a techno-scientific epoch:

All was well established, especially during the Gothic period. So an archi-tect in those days was pretty well furnished with everything in the way of ideas he needed to work with. He didn't have to be a *creator*. He merely had to be a sentient artist, with fine perception let's say and some prac-tical knowledge of building, especially if he was going to engage in some monumental enterprise. But he didn't have to *create* as he must do now.

We live under entirely different conditions. We live by this leverage we call the Machine. Most of us are machines ourselves; not much higher in consciousness and mentality than the man in the garage. Anyhow, *we do live by the machine* and we do have the enormous product of all modern sciences in our toolbox.

But as a matter of fact it is Science that is ruining us in Architecture and Art as it has already ruined Religion, as it has made a monkey of Philosophy. Already Science has practically destroyed us spiritually and is sending us into perpetual war.[10]

With *Genius and the Mobocracy* [pages 110–111], published under the sign of Wright's "red square" by Duell, Sloan and Pearce in 1949, the wheel came full circle, and Wright at the age of seventy-two returned once again to the time he spent in the Auditorium Building as "a pencil in the hand of the master." Written ostensibly as a gloss on a set of drawings Louis Sullivan had presented to Wright on April 11, 1924, just three days before Sullivan's death, *Genius and the Mobocracy* strayed from its ostensible subject in the usual Wrightian fashion before settling down to give an extremely personal account of the trials and tribulations of Sullivan's life — from the time he returned home from the École in Paris, as a "Parisite" (note the typical Wrightian pun), to his death at the age of sixty-eight. Much, as usual, floats to the surface in this text that is partly extraneous to the theme of the book — from the crucial importance of Nature as the source of all tectonic form as opposed to the eclecticism of History to the incapacity of photography to capture the essence of spatial depth. And the text is as much a sympathetic portrait of Dankmar Adler as an homage to Sullivan. We learn a good deal here about what it was like to live through the triumphant realization of the Adler and Sullivan Auditorium Building in 1890 and about how Sullivan, thereafter swollen-headed by his triumph at the age of thirty-four, would absent himself from the office for long periods of time and with increasing frequency. "The master was working away in his rose garden down there at Biloxi by the Gulf, next door to his beloved friends, the James Charnleys, for whom I had drawn a cottage which I liked better than lieber-meister's. Both were experiments that seem tame enough now. Later I designed the Charnley townhouse on Astor Street."

Needless to say, we learn as much about Wright and his young colleagues in the Sullivan orbit as we do about the master himself; above all we are told of George Elmslie's all but saint-like fidelity to Sullivan, even in his later years, and about the open competition — not to say confrontation — that developed almost at once between Wright and Irving Gill, leading to the latter's prompt departure after having been insulted by Wright. We are also provided with a brief but touching portrait of the young German engineer Paul Mueller from Stuttgart, who shortly passed from Sullivan's employ to become the engineering partner at Probst Construction, a firm that later realized a great deal of Wright's own work. Indeed, Wright was not beyond criticizing Sullivan for his misrepresentation of the presence of the steel frame in the elevations of the Wainwright Building — a critique that could be extended by implication to Wright's own high-rise exercise projected for the San Francisco Call Company in 1912, a work that Wright remained inordinately proud of throughout his life. However ultimately appreciative, Wright's criticism of Sullivan did not stop here, for as Wright declared, "It is only fair to say, now, that in none of these Adler and Sullivan buildings are 'form and function' one or, excepting clay (called terra cotta), is the nature-of-materials considered at all, either as a matter of fact or as determining organic form." This is Wright as the tectonic architect par excellence—an architect who like Augustus Pugin and Auguste Perret before him believed that materiality, structure, and construction were the absolute prerequisites for a great building culture. As he put it in *Genius and the Mobocracy*, "When I speak of architecture as organic, I mean the great art of structure coming back to its early integrity: again alive as a great reality."

Notes

1. Frank Lloyd Wright, "Wake Up America!," October 12, 1940, item 2401.242, version A, The Frank Lloyd Wright Foundation Archives (The Museum of Modern Art | Avery Architectural and Fine Arts Library, Columbia University, New York).
2. Wright, "Wake Up America!."
3. Frank Lloyd Wright, "The New Frontier: Broadacre City," *Taliesin*, vol. 1, no.1 (October 1940); reprinted in Bruce Brooks Pfeiffer, ed., *Frank Lloyd Wright: Collected Writings*, vol. 4 (New York: Rizzoli, 1992), 45–66.
4. Frank Lloyd Wright, "Book Five: Form," *An Autobiography*, 2nd ed. (New York: Duell, Sloan and Pearce, 1943), 402–432.
5. Frank Lloyd Wright, "Usonia, Usonia South and New England," August 24, 1941, item 2401.254, version D, The Frank Lloyd Wright Foundation Archives.
6. Robert Moses, "Mr. Moses Dissects the 'Long Haired Planners': The Park Commissioner Prefers Common Sense to Their Revolutionary Theories," *New York Times Magazine*, June 25, 1944; reprinted in Pfeiffer, *Frank Lloyd Wright: Collected Writings*, vol. 4, 298.
7. Frank Lloyd Wright, "Prejudice, Sir, Is a Disease," June 12, 1947, item 2401.287, version G, The Frank Lloyd Wright Foundation Archives.
8. Frank Lloyd Wright, "The Architect," in *The Works of the Mind* (Chicago: University of Chicago Press, 1947); reprinted in Pfeiffer, *Frank Lloyd Wright: Collected Writings*, vol. 4, 285.
9. Frank Lloyd Wright, "AIA Gold Medal Acceptance Speech" printed in the *Journal of the American Institute of Architects*, May 1949, item 2401.291, version A, The Frank Lloyd Wright Foundation Archives.
10. Wright, "AIA Gold Medal Acceptance Speech."

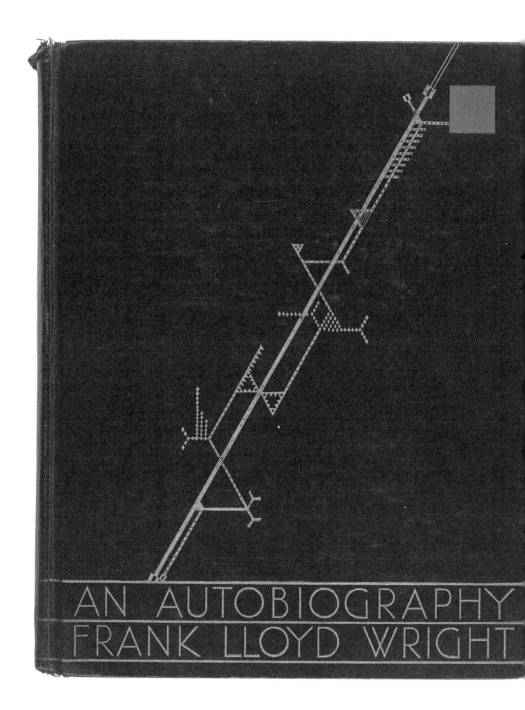

AN AUTOBIOGRAPHY
FRANK LLOYD WRIGHT

The first edition of *An Autobiography*, published by Longman's, Green and Co. in New York and London, 1932. The book was published again in an extended form by Duell, Sloan and Pearce in New York, 1943. In in the later edition, Wright added a final section, entitled "Book Five: Form."

WAKE UP AMERICA!

Our country's most creative minds have been shut out of
any decisive vote in the coming election by the bi-party
pact "to save Britian". As the current of nationalism now
runs to murder, any plan for the defense of our way of life
according to our best genius has been handed over to the
worm's eye view of war, prolonging war toward the ruin of the
way of life we could and should defend otherwise.

By way of popular "easements" (we call them publicity)
we have again been newsed, radioed and scared out of
democracy. During the several months just past I could listen
or read at any time anywhere and imagine myself back in the
stupid days of 1914. But that previous catastrophe to the
economy and morale of our world was nothing compared to what
now has us in its grip. Shame enough to sell out our best thought
at the first sign of danger and see our nationals running
pell-mell to play a second hand imitation of the enemy. Our
power can not lie in saving empire unless we too are empirical.
Imitation is always base and never yet won a battle. Our
real enemy is not Hitler. The real enemy of Democracy lies
in our own timidity and stupidity as seen in this frightful
current smoothly moved or waxed in the direction of self
destruction "to save Britian"? To maintain Britian as our
only shield against slavery or destruction is the insane
notion sold to mediocrity by way of its own salesmen from the
chief executive himself down to the journalistic horde. The
only safe-guard Democracy can have is a free, morally enlightened,
fearless minority. Unfortunately for our country such enlighten-

NO INSTITUTES
NO PETTY OFFICIALISM
NO LANDLORD————————NO TENANT
NO POLITICIANS——NO ACADEMICIANS
NO TRAFFIC PROBLEM
NO BACK AND FORTH HAUL
NO POLES————————NO WIRES IN SIGHT
NO DITCHES ALONGSIDE THE ROADS
NO HEADLIGHTS——NO VISIBLE LAMPS
NO POLICEMEN
NO MINOR AXIS——NO MAJOR AXIS
NO YARDS FOR RAW MATERIALS
NO SMOKE————————NO HARDRAILS
NO RADIO OR BILLBOARD ADVERTISING
NO SLUM————————————NO SCUM

"Tenets of Broadacre City" from *Taliesin*, vol. 1, no. 1 (October 1940).

USONIA, USONIA SOUTH AND NEW ENGLAND

Here in our national home the atmosphere is becoming so heated, so loaded
with false implications and impurities, now so close that any voice telling
truth is like an open window letting in fresh air. Already the open-window is
regarded as a danger, so our windows are shut or obscured by fear. An
independent is named an Isolationist and patriotism is degraded to a level where no
true patriot would stand, where a convoy becomes a patrol.

Never during our national life-time have evil influences of foreign interests
upon the natives so pervaded out national living-room as now. Never have the
windows been so obscured nor doors so well bolted -- from the outside! The doors
were first slammed shut by undemocratic preelection concord between F.D.R. and
W.W. one of whom was elected by the people on a promise that is becoming manifest
as a lie.

With this elected president cheerfully making a role for himself never intended
for the president of this republic, in any circumstances whatsoever, the role of
ruler, we the people of this country, unable to see clearly, are sinking deeper
into fatal coma -- we are less and less able to recognize ourselves as a free,
independent nation. Instead of honest forthright independence, all we know is what
we read in the papers and all the papers know is what they think is good for the
people to know in the circumstances.

We are now dependents in order that a "ruler" may make a bid for world-power and
for commercial-supremacy. Both were, and always will be, a despot's mirage.

"Usonia, Usonia South and New England," published in *Taliesin Square-Paper:
A Nonpolitical Voice from Our Democratic Minority*, no. 6 (August 24, 1941). The
piece, which outlines Wright's vision for reorganizing the US into a three-state
federal union, begins with a statement on national sentiment: "Already the
open-window is regarded as a danger, so our windows are shut or obscured
by fear."

A Taliesin Square-Paper: A Nonpolitical Voice from Our Democratic Minority, no. 1 (May 15, 1941), shown here in its unfolded form. Published and printed by The Taliesin Press in Spring Green, Wisconsin; the edition held by Avery Library is addressed to Serge Chermayeff.

A TALIESIN SQUARE-PAPER
A NONPOLITICAL VOICE FROM
OUR DEMOCRATIC MINORITY

"EARLESS ENLIGHTENED MINORITY IS THE CONSCIENCE OF A DEMOCRATIC NATION.
IS STIFLED, DEMOCRACY IS GONE FROM THE LIFE OF THE PEOPLE AND FROM THE
HE NATION."

Serge Chermayeff,
3515 Robinson Drive,
Oakland,
California.

NO. 2
MAY
1941

101

OF WHAT USE IS A GREAT NAVY WITH NO PLACE T

HITLER IS WINNING THIS WAR WITHOUT A NAVY. We are facing a new kind of wa
British Empire, owing to traditional faith in a great navy, cannot learn in time even if we
equipment. We couldn't furnish the equipment because we don't yet know how to mai
to Britain is impossible except to prolong the death agony of a great empire. Meanwhile
erately weakening our own chance of survival if and when our time comes. Our frontier
England nor, in any sense, is it European. Our frontier is our own shores. And the shorter
the better. Any realistic view of what goes on in Europe must make this plain to all but exp
and news-sheet strategists. This war cannot be won on the sea. War has shifted its ce

England needed a strong friend and we might have been that strong friend to Eng
have failed her as the Empire in desperation has now failed so many nations. A libera
and moderate democratic nationalist myself, I am no believer in world - conquest nor hav
in so-called world-power. I hate the thought of Empire.

So long as I am governed by my choice of government I concede to others their rig
erned as they choose to be governed. I will prepare to defend this, my right, as their rig
fight only when attacked. If this were lived up to honestly by us as a nation our United
be impregnable and we would be a fatal stumbling block in the path of any plan
conquest" either from within or from without. Because I honestly believe in democracy
form of world-power or sea-control both dated and doomed.

The shift in the center of warfare is in our favor. But once actually committed to E
we are a bygone tradition ourselves.

Our danger lies not so much in far-reaching German Geopolitik as in the fact that th
of our leader nods, taxed beyond human endurance. He has lost common-sense and to
people in the arduous decisions of a rash third term. He sees himself the vis-a-vis of Hi
country a hinterland growing dim.

Our danger lies in the fact that our best belligerents know so little of the world forces
in purely imaginary self-defense, and wish to see conquered in order that we may call ther
ocratic." A complete loss of perspective.

Our danger lies in the publicity-politics of frightened interests that have no genuine
from which to determine what or how we should fight if we fought: able to think only
billions of dollars at a time when all dollars are on the way down and out.

Our danger lies in perpetually propagated advertising slogans that amount to lies fed i
by newsheet and radio, lest the people use their common sense. All, so help me God, in
democracy! The worst element in our body politic, as usual, becoming the most "patriotic."

And, of course, not only our danger but our end as a democratic nation lies in any o
soever to take over this world-war on foreign shores. We have nothing to take over
deflated dollars, conscript green cannon-fodder, and a vast, already dated, arsenal on ore

Well, again coming home across the hinterland, I see vast empty spaces of good gr
ing occasional gas-stations and auto-camps opportunity to testify to our great country
backward empty-place. but l . . made ready to go to other shores to fight for something
got at home, som . . . . to be found at home if it is ever to be found at all. I

1

money-makers to . . . . nders. And we see it coming clearer every day tha
use in being mon . . . . onger if Empire, the apotheosis of money, is going dowr

And we see that if we would save Empire, we the democratic people must go to wi
we can't save Empire everybody, the money spenders especially, must go to work. No
work shouldn't seem so bad even in the kind of democracy we think we are. But to that
of us that is already an out-and-out pseudo-fascist empire reflecting the great disappe
empire, the thing must look fearful and hateful enough.

The democratic people must know, at heart, that going to war is the natural basi
Going to War is a lot easier than going to work, for all but the boys who are to kill or be
or be maimed. And the spenders know how to make, even that, exciting to the boys: lo
gilt buttons, gilt broid, brass bands, fine horses, great battleships, big forts and guns and
dated but still picturesque paraphernalia including pocket money and medals for brave
in camp, etc. Meantime papas and mamas throbbing and sobbing with pride, grief
church bells ringing—preachers preaching, sweethearts exciting, the news-sheets citing. A
again on the well-worn bloody trail to Nowhere and Never. Forever.

Why does the damned thing keep on working? Is it because Work as an Ideal
Life has gone heavy and stale and Money is now the universal means that has already supe
to achieve the supreme reward?

No. In a democracy we won't give up so easily. We can be flim-flammed for a
boozled a good deal—but I still believe we are more intelligent than we were last big
And I believe that as a whole we the democratic people of this nation love the ideal of a
well enough to go to work for it, even for wages. But how much better instead of going
wages to go to work for ourselves on our own ground in our own way? Silly as it may
cited and inciting authority just now that is our new frontier—that and cooperative manufa
merchandising. Hitler could not cross that Frontier.

Policies can never supplant principles for long though the beautiful people are 'c
deviled and debauched by the prevailing conspiracy of newsheet lies, radio talks and phon
words for wage-labor and for conventional moral conduct. No—all this can not obscu
issue. Because this nation keeps sound at heart if the face does get dirty. And I say it is
at home, our common decency, that keeps the children clean, well-dressed and on the
district school: our married folk keeping decently together to keep a pleasant home to
free to be honest with themselves and each other and all others;—hating (as I believe most o
tiful people" do hate) the hypocrisy that goes with all these money-standards that are driv
idea of life crazy and are now trying so hard to waste the whole future of a great new r
other phoney war; on the lips the same hypocrisy that we inherited; and a conscience using
ad nauseum, high sounding slogans for any and every dirty expedient. I say this, our com
at home is our best national asset. If it got a fair break.

. . . .

America! Wake up! The tragedy that will be our doom lies in the fact that such hyp
conceals, even from itself, that the worm's eye view of war is past; this hypocrisy conceal

3

"Of What Use Is a Great Navy with No Place to Hide?" in *A Taliesin Square-Paper: A Nonpolitical Voice from Our Democratic Minority*, no. 1 (May 15, 1941). Published and printed by The Taliesin Press in Spring Green, Wisconsin. Written eight months before Pearl Harbor, Wright, almost prophetically, expressed his opposition to US intervention in World War II.

night be worth-while if only we could get that something (call it democratic prosperity) and
k with us. Of course we won't get it that way, but fear does funny things to the human
can raise a hue and cry. It can. The hue and cry is rising and the same old funny
eing done to us, right now, in the same old name of patriotism and democracy. Yes,
ng up our native land by way of an over-stressed president who now says it is "over
f we want it we will have to go over there to get it. There is a limit to the important
y human being can make. Evidently our president is fagged or bogged down to reflect
pkins, Wendell Willkie, Hull, Stimson, and Knox, amateur strategists all, some of whom
broad quite recently but also others, hangovers from early days still trying to keep our
s loyal English colonies.
. . . our President says "It"—Democracy—is "over there" and we must go over there to save
e" meaning Dakar, Suez, Abbysinia, Singapore, Egypt, Greece, Finland, Norway, Holland,
nmark, France—to all and sundry of whom (we will say nothing of Spain and the others) he
urances of support even as the great Empire has given to all and sundry, promises of mili-
rinciple being utterly lacking in all this we can only turn to policy to account for it. If we
e find only the policy found in a good old U.S.A. game: the good old game of poker.
ying poker with no cards in the hand above a two spot and the joker is not "policy" at all.
ther name for it, out there in the barn.
William Allen White found he was in with a lot of gangsters making war-whoopee he got
say he got out just in time to save himself as we know him. But Will still believes that the
keep the great Empire up against Warrior Germany, the less able Germany will be to mo-
d so Will is for all out aid to the great Empire, short of war, as an American shield. Just as
has been doing that same thing to seven or eight other nations—British "shields" that have
. Willing to fight to the last Englishman then, is it our turn?
itude may be pre-eminently British, but it is utterly not American. This little fellow who hides
big fellow's back is not so much nobler than the big fellow who hides behind the little fellow.

merican politics as played at present, imitating English politics, is a sorry equivocation with
ment of honest democracy in it. I can see nothing even decent in this frightened nations
ng itself to give a pell-mell imitation of the great Empire.
an't we, the democratic people, see that the weakness of the Great Empire lies in the fact
ated if not senile and see for ourselves that it is no longer a great power? And see the
ly going beyond the fetich of great Empire either commercial, moral, or real-estate. The
people must see that Empire is no more than the apotheosis of Money and see the world
ng to realize that work is the miracle—not money. Work can do without money if it has
leadership. Money can't do without work no matter what leadership it has unless it can
nd go to war. Therein (at last) is really where this world-struggle simmers down for us in
d States. Tell our democratic people that truth! I say, tell them that where we are concerned
ng tragedy is going to lie in the fact that our enemies champion work while we champion
the great would-be democracy caught on the wrong side of the economic problem, and now
dy to fight to keep on being wrong!
 well our universities have done their work! They have tried to make the beautif

t that to cling for salvation to out-moded engines of destruction like battleships, infantry,
forts, whether floating or forever fixed, is to cling for salvation to pure illusion. We the
eople in these United States should see that the new agencies of our future were they
with ideas and labor, not money, would be better able to protect life than ever those new
e or ever will be able to destroy it? Yet here again in all this our nation is setting itself aside,
o the advice of military experts, but ordered about by politicians, resorting again to out-
ngines just as obsolete as the horse and buggy and the urban manure pile. "National de-
unable to see that this nation's defense no longer consists in fool man-toys that modern
lready rendered useless to the future. It is the democratic people themselves who must see
defense and salvation lie ahead of these United States of America in ordered decentraliza-
l reintegration with the ground, in a natural capitalist economy: in effective solidarity of
purpose to grow independent and strong here at home.
cause we have run out of good ideas do we want to fight.
old order rises again like a ghoul from the grave to reach the sap in our veins. If it is
conscription and war it will be solely because we the democratic people are too proud of
and shop to learn to see Reality anew. We stated that reality ourselves when we were our-
not so long ago. Reality will be ours again. A great upsurge of rensentment against the
ied to push this war over on us is going to rise from our soil and popular anger will sweep
with disastrous results—when the "beautiful people" find out how they have been lied to
for what purpose.
ngland but I hate Empire as much as the more enlightened English people themselves hate
y I deplore the weakness that cannot stand against it with the better English thought of to-

say to our own beautiful people . . . . hell—let's be ourselves. Yes, if we die for it. To
than living as a cheap imitation of something that should have died a natural death of en-
a half century ago instead of being now forced to its knees or to a bloody disgraceful end.

Wright : Taliesin
?41

TO WAR THE ONLY WAY THE UNITED STATES CAN MEET AN ENEMY TO ITS PRINCIPLES?

A TALIESIN SQUARE-PAPER
A NONPOLITICAL VOICE FROM
OUR DEMOCRATIC MINORITY

"A FREE FEARLESS ENLIGHTENED MINORITY IS THE CONSCIENCE OF A DEMOCRATIC NATION. WHEN IT IS STIFLED, DEMOCRACY IS GONE FROM THE LIFE OF THE PEOPLE AND FROM THE LIFE OF THE NATION."

Sec. 562 P. L. & R.

A Taliesin Square-Paper: A Nonpolitical Voice from Our Democratic Minority, no. 3 (May 29, 1941). Published and printed by The Taliesin Press in Spring Green, Wisconsin.

THE FOLLOWING TEXT, AN EXCHANGE BETWEEN MYSELF AND WILLIAM T. EVJUE, EDITOR, IS REPRO-DUCED FROM THE CAPITAL TIMES OF MADISON, WISCONSIN, THURSDAY, MAY 29TH, 1941. A SECOND ARTICLE REPLYING TO THE ACCUSATION HE HAD MADE THAT, PRESSED FOR A BETTER PLAN THAN THE PRESIDENT'S I HAD BEEN ONLY "VAGUE", WAS PRINTED IN THE TIMES, FRIDAY, JUNE 6TH, 1941. A FRIENDLY GIBE AT THE THOUGHT OF AMERICAS SALVATION COMING FROM THE GREEN HILLS OF TAL-IESIN WAS HIS CONCLUSION.

GOOD AFTERNOON, EDITOR EVJUE:

I have great respect and considerable affection for the editor of this paper. The fact that I deplore the violence of his anti-Hitlerism does not diminish this fact.

Deploring the extremity of his anti-Hitlerism does not mean that I am pro-Nazi. It means that I think he is trying to shoot the weathervane off the steeple when the congregation in the church below is his real enemy. And I admire his loyalty to our president because he believes the president's foreign policy is right. He is fortunate. I believe the president's foreign policy is dangerously wrong so I can only say so honestly. I am unfortunate. There is no need for me to say that I believe every Nazi utterly wrong for our United States because every principle I advocate, every act of my life is by nature, as I am myself, anti-Nazi.

Believing in democracy, however, I fail to see what right we have as a nation to say to that nation or any other nation, "You are all wet. Get democratic or we'll blow you out of the water—or to hell and gone with you before you get us." I can look with perfect confidence and calm upon a world entirely undemocratic provided I and my friendly neighbors, if I happen to have any such, are not directly molested. And if undemocratic ways of living and making a living are not forced upon me where I live.

The problem of meeting any threat of that kind I should say should not be met by abandoning what I believed in to get tough with the propective enemy but by meeting him with actual proofs that my democratic faith and way of life was a better way than his way, were the enemy fascist, communist, empirical or capitalist. For the life of me I can't see how I could show that to an enemy by imitating his own faults and committing murder to match his own murdering.

Nor can I believe in Franklin Roosevelt's placing himself vis-a-vis with Hitler as the self-appointed saviour of the world. I don't believe in a saviour of the world. If I did I don't know what right he would have to save it from itself unless it appealed to him for salvation. It has not and probably will not, now. The world might have done so once upon a time, before Franklin made us a mere accomplice. England, however, has appealed to us for salvation and if the English dominion itself were in danger and had openly declared for democratic-government instead of kingly-empire I should be inclined to give neighborly aid. But even then I should not jeopardize my home and my people's future by deliberately setting my own house on fire trying to put out the fire in the house appealing for aid. Etc. Etc. Etc. Etc.

I am as "British" as they ought to make them in these United States. I have been greatly honored by the British nation but I do not think that a sufficient reason for me to abandon my principles or see my nation's welfare jeopardized without protest. It may be that I owe all this backwardness to lack of an early education at Groton under Dr. Peabody and a subsequent confirmation at Harvard. Unfortunately I am a native product from the tall grass of our midwestern pra-

1

"Good Afternoon, Editor Evjue," in *A Taliesin Square-Paper: A Nonpolitical Voice from Our Democratic Minority*, no. 3 (May 29, 1941). The piece was originally published in *The Capital Times* as a response to editor William T. Evjue on US non-involvement in the war.

105

D E F E N S E

No matter by what evidence the truth may be confronted, mankind in these
United States is more individualized from day to day.   Men are getting more
and more concerned for their individuality. They do take increasing pride
in the personal element. Universality is, therefore, losing importance and
power as quality rises above quantity. Notwithstanding such success as we
are seeing in European warfare, *AND AMERICAN BIG-BUSINESS* general formulae do prove themselves increasingly
insufficient in human affairs as destruction, *AND INANE WEALTH* gains headway.   Human significance
is more and more revealed to the individual by the individual in more and
more highly specialized forms because "God becomes mightier in the process".
And now, we the people of these United States should stop this vain bluffing
with out-moded arms, *MURDER MACHINES* and begin to defend ourselves permanently by building *PREPARE*
up defense from the beginning, *ON A SOLID FOUNDATION.* Build defense as straight forward as possible.
Build up our own peculiar strength as single mindedly from within as it is
possible for us to build it.   And build as unconcerned for everything remote
or external as we can. The more we do this as individuals the purer and stronger
we will become as a united people championing human Freedom.   The less we
ally ourselves with alien forces; and the less we rely upon them, *THESE FORCES;* the more
we take of ourselves upon our own shoulders; the more nature will smile *UPON* on us
in our effort to build an impregnable free nation.   Our true defense is
not military now nor will be ever if we know the truth about ourselves. Let this
truth come through: Democracy is far stronger than Fascism or Communism or any
other ism if allowed to work.   The idea of the absolute autonomy of a free man
has created a power in this world mightier than anything that can be opposed
to it!

"Defense," published in *A Taliesin Square-Paper: A Nonpolitical Voice from Our Democratic Minority*, no. 4 (July 4, 1941).

WHEN DEMOCRACY BUILDS

AND THOU, AMERICA . . . .

Thou, too, surroundest all,
Embracing, carrying, welcoming all, thou too
By pathways broad and new approach the Ideal.

The measured faiths of other lands,
The grandeurs of the past, are not for thee,
But grandeurs of thine own,
Deific faiths and amplitudes, absorbing, comprehending all,
All in all to all.

Give me, O God, to sing that thought,
Give me, give him or her I love this quenchless faith in Thee.
Whatever else withheld withhold not from us
Belief in plan of Thee enclosed in Time and Space . . . .

Fragment transcribed from Walt Whitman

When Democracy Builds, published in Chicago by University of Chicago Press, 1945.

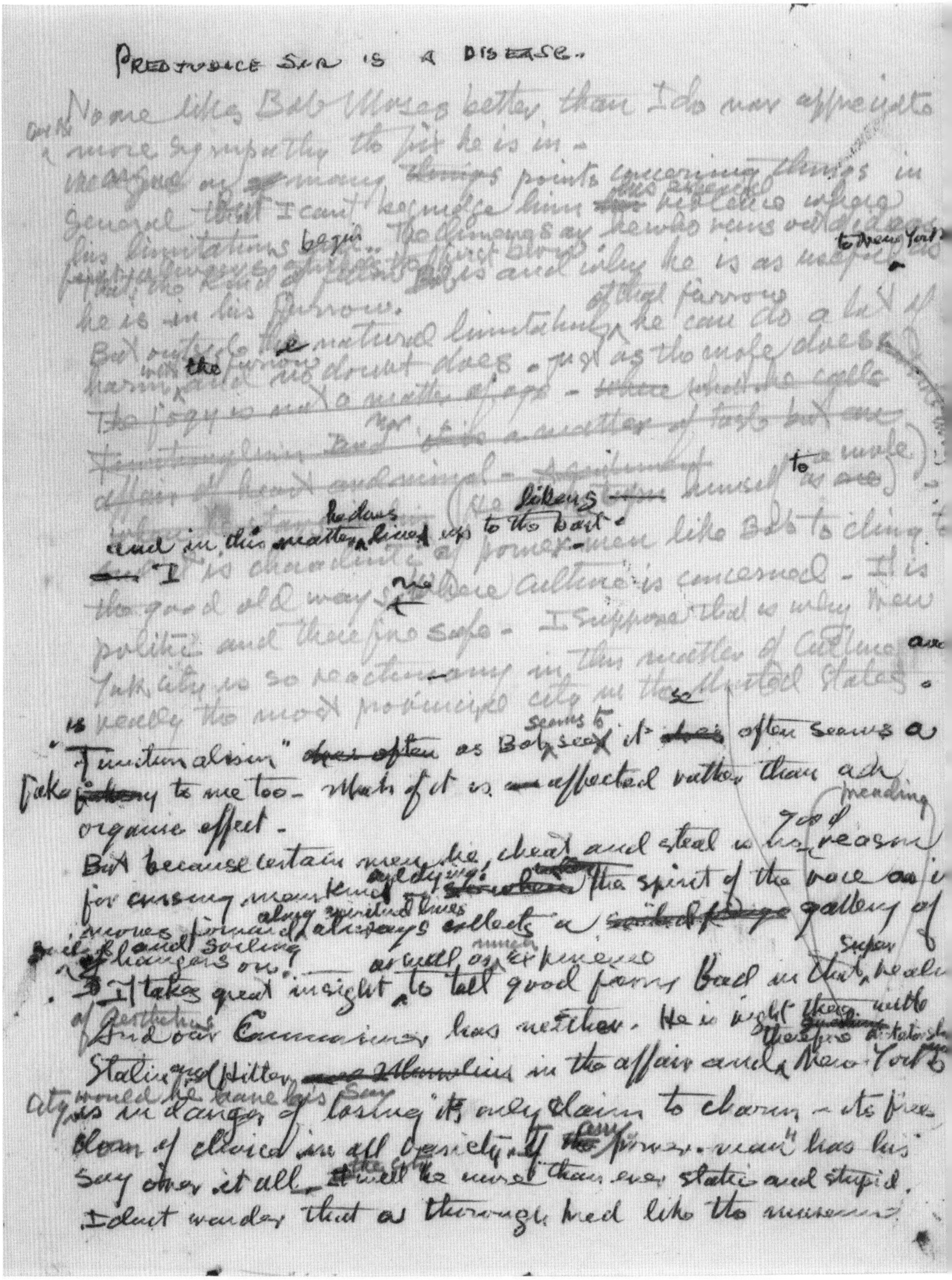

PREJUDICE SIR IS A DISEASE.

None likes Bob Moses better than I do nor appreciate more sympathy the fix he is in - [illegible]

[illegible]

"Functionalism" is as Bob seems to see it often seems a fake to me too - much of it is affected rather than an organic effect.

[illegible]

Stalin and Hitler [illegible] in the affair and New York city is in danger of losing its only claim to charm - its freedom of choice in all variety. If any "power-view" has his say over it all, the city will be worse than ever static and stupid. I don't wonder that as thorough-bred like the museum [illegible]

“Prejudice, Sir, Is a Disease,” 1947; the piece, intended as an affront to Robert Moses, criticizes the provincialism of New York’s master builder.

ture, Western Reserve University, Cleveland, Ohio, received a citation for distinguished service to his profession from the Cleveland Chapter, A.I.A. The occasion was his twenty-fifth anniversary as Dean of the School which was started by the Chapter in 1923.

Acceptance Speech of Frank Lloyd Wright

hearing the president's citation and

UPON RECEIVING THE GOLD MEDAL ~~FOR~~

~~For~~ 1948 OF THE *at the* AMERICAN INSTITUTE OF ARCHITECTS, RICE HOTEL, HOUSTON, TEXAS,
MARCH 17, 1949

this really fine citation.

Mr President – I thank you.

LADIES AND GENTLEMEN:

No man climbs so high or sinks so low that he isn't eager to receive the good will and admiration of his fellowmen. He may be reprehensible in many ways; he may seem to care nothing about it; he may hitch his wagon to his star and, however he may be circumstanced or whatever his ideals or his actions, he never loses the desire for the approbation of his kind.

So I feel humble and grateful. I don't think humility is a very becoming state for me, but I really feel touched by this token of esteem from the home boys. It has reached me from almost every great nation in the world. It's been a long time coming from home. But here it is at last, and very handsomely indeed. And I am extremely grateful. • • • • •

I don't know what change it's going to effect upon my course in the future. It is bound to have an effect. I am not going to be the same man when I walk out of here that I was when I came in. Be-

cause, by this little token in my pocket, it seems to me that a battle has been won.

I felt that way when I was sitting in my little home in Arizona in '41, and the news came over the wire that the Gold Medal of the Royal Institute of British Architects had fallen to a lad out there in the Middle West, in the tall grass. Well, I felt then that the youngsters who have held, we will say, with me and who have believed and made sacrifices and taken the gaff with me, had won a world-wide fight. But it had'nt been won at home. The Cape Cod Colonial—by the way, have any of you observed what we fellows have done to the Colonial? Have you seen it come down, and its front open to the weather, and the wings extend, and have it become more and more reconciled to the ground? It has; you notice it.

Well, anyway, it is very unbecoming on an occasion like this to boast. But I do want to say something that may account in a meas-

199

110   *Genius and the Mobocracy*, published by Duell, Sloan and Pearce
in New York, 1949.

1949–1959

As is invariably the case with one of mature years, Wright had long been in the habit of repeating himself. Throughout the 1950s Wright reworked familiar ground, remonstrating in general with the failed promise of civilization and reacting sharply from time to time to the minor incidents or major disasters of the day. In *The Architectural Forum* of April 1951, Wright expressed his despair at the increasing mechanization of everyday life and at the onslaught of its ever escalating speed. In the face of this, he urged the youth of his time to strengthen themselves by embracing the Buddhist doctrine of tranquility. Elsewhere he belabored the reader with his pet anathemas, from his total contempt for all forms of speculation to his unremitting repudiation of urban congestion.

In the early 1950s, Wright returned to his enthusiasm for Eugène Viollet-le-Duc and to his simultaneous condemnation of both the Renaissance and the International Style, seeing the latter as part of the same classicizing impulse running forward from the middle of the fifteenth century to the present. As he put it, after Victor Hugo, "The Renaissance in Europe — a setting sun that all Europe mistook for a dawn." In this regard his critical position was close to that of Augustus Pugin or even, paradoxically, to that of his contemporary Auguste Perret, who in other respects could be disregarded as a classicist.

Wright was also honored in the early 1950s both nationally and internationally with a large retrospective exhibition of his work that traveled throughout Europe, displaying his unquestioned brilliance in one prestigious venue after another, beginning, ironically enough, with the Palazzo Strozzi in Florence and passing from there to the Kunsthaus in Zürich—one of the few modern buildings in Europe that Wright unequivocally admired. In numerous valedictory letters sent to distinguished architects all over the world at this time, one senses that Wright was only too aware that this was almost certainly his last public appearance as the architect of the century. In these letters he reaffirmed, once again, his lifelong respect for both the German and Japanese cultures and his lasting debt to the Netherlands for having been one of the first countries to accord him public recognition. He also acknowledged the sympathetic visit he received from Hendrik Petrus Berlage as early as 1911, to be followed by other distinguished Dutch architects, most notably the neoplasticist Robert van't Hoff and Hendrikus Th. Wijdeveld, the editor of *Wendingen* magazine, which in 1925 published five special issues dedicated solely to Wright's work.

Wright's retrospective, designed by Oscar Stonorov and entitled *Sixty Years of Living Architecture*, originated at Gimbels in Philadelphia and traveled to Italy, Switzerland, France, Germany, Holland, and Mexico. It was an international celebration of Wright's heroic career on a grand scale, and Wright was understandably gratified by all the attention he received as a result: citations, medals, and special issues published by five different magazines around the world.

In the occasional essays of his last decade Wright was often at his most interesting when dealing with unlikely themes, as in his review of Edwin Lutyens's *Memorial Volumes* edited by Christopher Hussey [page 120], wherein, understandably enough, he preferred the Arts and Crafts Lutyens to the "Wrenaissance" of his Viceroy's Palace in New Delhi. The period saw Wright again condemning American militarism, only this time the cause célèbre was the Korean War and the accompanying American paranoia about the threat of Communist domination. In his short, journalistic piece "Wake Up, Wisconsin" [page 121] Wright again chided the American public for their political immaturity: "Do they really know what Communism means? Ask them. Their answers will make you laugh. Do they know what democracy means? Ask them and weep." Wright's loathing of totalitarianism was answered by his vehement antipathy to demagogy. Thus his tolerant attitude toward the Soviet Union, aided no doubt by Olgivanna's empathy for all things Russian, was matched by his simultaneous detestation for the witch hunt that was then being so ardently pursued by Senator Joseph McCarthy, to which Wright was by no means immune.

Toward the end of his life Wright became even less tolerant of what he regarded as totalitarianism in architecture, namely the so-called International Style. Hence the endless diatribe against the orthogonal box that came to the fore once again in 1952 in a piece entitled "Organic Architecture Looks at Modern Architecture" [pages 122–123]. This critique was followed by an essay in which he came out against proselytizers of all kinds, from the so-called "big three" of the Yalta Conference to the superimposition of Bauhaus values on American culture. It is strange to find Wright divided at this juncture between his lifelong admiration of Germany and the total disdain he felt for the émigré functionalists of the Weimar Republic—above all for Mies van der Rohe and his scandalous "less is more" slogan, and Walter Gropius, who while remaining unnamed, was the director of a major East Coast "plan factory" (a term Wright disdainfully used to refer to all university schools of architecture). Condemning Mies for having reduced architecture to nothing more than a dematerialized skeleton, Wright attacked the curtain-walled, freestanding slab, particularly as it appeared in the United Nations building in New York in 1952—an institution Wright blithely denounced out of hand for being more fascist than democratic. Although neither the Unité d'Habitation in Marseille nor Le Corbusier are ever mentioned by name, they are surely the double target of an odd essay entitled "Massacre on the Marseilles Waterfront." Elsewhere Wright reasserted his belief that ornament must be *of* the thing and not *on* it and that only through adhering to this precept is it possible to enhance the character of a building through ornament.

In a further attack on the Museum of Modern Art for its internationalism, Wright argued that if an intrinsic architecture failed to emerge in the United States, the country would never have a culture of its own. For Wright, only individual creativity could guarantee, as it were, the emergence of an independent, native, American culture as opposed to what he saw as left-wing standardization in the work of Mies van der Rohe. This unremitting critique of the Bauhaus movement was to be pursued by Wright throughout the 1950s in one text after another.

The Natural House [page 125], written in 1954, is also largely a reworking of Wright's previous writings. The initial chapter on organic architecture first appeared in 1936 in the British *The Architect's Journal*, and both chapters "Building the New House" and "In the Nature of Materials" were taken straight from his autobiography. Only a lengthy essay at the end, "Concerning the Usonian House," had in fact been expressly written for the occasion. All in all, Wright was at his non-rhetorical best on the theme of this elegant paradigm which in the last analysis was perhaps the most "democratic" invention. Despite the fact that it was never as widely adopted as he would have liked, the Usonian House, in all its guises, still remains the last serious attempt on the part of an American architect to render the suburb as a place of cultivation. In *The Natural House*, Wright's intelligence reveals itself with refreshing directness. Once he abandoned the repetitive, recalcitrant tone that characterizes so much of his writing, Wright was able to convey to the reader the raison d'être of the Usonian prototype extremely persuasively. However, in advising his Broadacre clients to build as far from the city as possible, he overlooked the fact that there was little to support his contention that "We have all the means to live free and independent, far apart — as we choose — [while] still retaining all the social relationships and advantages we ever had, even to have them multiplied." Apart from such inevitable grandiose assertions, *The Natural House* is leavened by the pragmatic advice throughout it — whether instructing the reader about the advantages of drywall footings or maintaining that artificial light should be provided in much the same way as natural light to avoid the unpleasant glare of spotlighting. Wright even defended the lack of sufficient insulation in the Usonian three-ply timber wall on the grounds that the most important thing was to keep one's feet warm, thereby simultaneously justifying both the thinness of the walls and his use of radiant floor heating. He went so far as to suggest that if it became very cold all one had to do was simply put on more clothes. To his credit Wright remained skeptical of the virtues of central air conditioning, particularly in private homes. He saw this as further evidence of the excesses of mechanization, which was both unhealthy and uneconomical.

Published in 1958, a year before his death, *The Living City* [pages 126–127] returns to the themes of *The Disappearing City* (1932). As in *The Natural House*, Wright cannibalized an earlier text — in this case the interim version of the Broadacre thesis from *When Democracy Builds* (1945). In many instances Wright did little more than change a word or subtitle here and there or rearrange the syntax. Reacting to earlier reviews in which he had been "accused," as he put it, with preposterous irony, of being unduly "Capitalistic," Wright responded by decapitalizing words throughout the text. All these rearrangements seem to have been employed simply to eliminate any grounds for legal action between the two publishers, who had become, as it were, ensnared in Wright's compulsive reiterations.

116

Between 1953 and his death in 1959 Wright produced a seemingly end-less stream of books and articles, including *The Future of Architecture* (1953) [page 124]; *An American Architecture* (1955), edited by Edgar Kaufman; *The Natural House* (1954); *The Story of the Tower* (1956); *A Testament* (1957); and *The Living City* (1958). Along with this rather self-serving output came two texts calm in tone and somehow fresh: the brief but lively gloss written for the beautiful photographic record of the Price Tower building in Bartlesville, Oklahoma, entitled *The Story of the Tower*, and the relaxed flow of somewhat distant but lucid reflections on his long and exceedingly rich life, simply entitled *A Testament*.

The Story of the Tower [pages 128–129] is compelling because of its specificity. It is a text written with the full enthusiasm of someone who had finally realized a work that he had dreamed of building for more than thirty years — certain aspects of the Price Tower date back, in tectonic terms, to his National Life Insurance Building, projected for Chicago in 1924. Here we read a description that could be applied word for word to the Chicago project:

> The steel textile, embedded in concrete, a machine age product of great value and beauty, here clothes interior space inside the glass and allows more light or less light, more or less privacy as desired under chang-ing conditions. All exposed surfaces of the building except the central mass and floors, the supporting structure itself, are of copper. Partitions and furniture are designed as one and fabricated in the shop. . . see the spider — steel — spinning its web to enmesh glass — glass clear — glass translucent — glass in relief — glass in color. Iridescent surfaces of this light-fabric rising high against the blue out of the whole city, the city now seen as a park, the metal fabrication of the shafts themselves turquoise or gold, silver, bronze; the glass surfaces between the threads of fabric shim-mering with light reflected, light refracted — sparkling light broken into imaginative patterns.[1]

As the text proceeds, his mind runs back to the use of long-span, structural steel in the Robie House and forward to his vision of the Broadacre City:

> This skyscraper, planned to stand free in an open park and thus be more fit for human occupancy. . . here doing for the tall building what Lidgerwood made steel to do for the long ship. The ship had its steel keel: this concrete building has its steel core. A composite shaft of concrete

rises through the floors, each slab engaging the floors at nineteen levels. Each floor proceeds outward from the shaft as a cantilever slab extended from the shaft, similar to the branch of a tree from its trunk. The slab, thick at the shaft, similar to the branch of a tree from its trunk. The slab, thick at the shaft, grows thinner as it goes outward in an overlapping scale pattern in concrete until at the final outer leap to the screen wall it is no more than 3 inches thick. The outer enclosing screens of glass and copper are pendent from the edge of the cantilever slabs. The inner partitions rest upon the slabs. . . But the building is so placed that the sun shines on only one wall at a time and narrow upright blades, or mullions, project nine inches so that as the sun moves, shadows fall on the glass surfaces and afford the protection necessary for comfort.

The building increases substantially in area from floor to floor as the structure rises, in order that the glass frontage of each story may drip clear of the one below, the building thus cleaning itself.[2]

Elsewhere, challenged no doubt by the technocratic theories of Richard Buckminster Fuller, Wright went so far as to proclaim proudly that his building weighed six-tenths as much as a steel-framed Art Deco skyscraper clad in masonry.

All in all, the reminiscent writing in A Testament [page 130] is too mellow to hold one's attention for long. Only now and then does Wright really bring us up short, as in the following unmitigated attack upon the totally corrupt state of American culture:

Meantime we boast the highest standard of living in the world, when it is only the biggest. Society finds itself helplessly committed to these excesses and pressures. Ugliness is inevitable to this inorganic, therefore senseless, waste motion of the precious life of our time become a form of involuntary homicide [sic]. So mesmerized are we by the "payoff" that any public participation in culture becomes likewise wasted. So little are we enlisted in the potential new life that belongs to America.

Thus cheated by ourselves of general culture we have little genuine architecture. Official authority being by nature more and more merely numerical is already helpless even to recognize this fact, basic as it is.[3]

He wrote elsewhere in the same text:

To what extent is the bureaucrat to determine the culture of our civilization? The "insolence of office" thrives upon conformity. See now the distortion of our intrinsic social purpose by experts and specialists and the encouragement of mediocrity by mass-education. With the inspiration of great art unheeded, where is the check to deterioration? Are architecture and art simply to fade out with religion?[4]

Despite this pessimism, *A Testament* ends on a positive note with a résumé of Wright's Usonian precepts and a documentation of his astounding mile-high skyscraper, otherwise known as The Illinois-Sky City, designed for Chicago. However we need only to read the science-fiction description of its atomic powered, mega-elevator system, rising for 528 floors, complemented by 150 helicopter landing pads cantilevering out from its progressively diminishing shaft, to realize how the proposal entailed levels of supra-mechanization that Wright himself would have totally abhorred in other circumstances.

Wright produced eight more occasional essays before his death at the age of ninety-one on April 9, 1959. Although he wrote to the very end, among his final pieces only one short essay, celebrating the imminent realization of the Guggenheim Museum, manifests his usual aplomb. It is just possible that this self-serving, eccentric polemic in favor of liberating painting from the tyranny of the rectilinear wall was in fact some kind of veiled instruction to the recalcitrant first director of the Guggenheim, James Johnson Sweeney, despite his hostility toward him, as to how he might intelligently exploit the full potential of the building. The remaining essays are written in a minor key and, despite relieving flashes of irony and wit, the overall tone is mordant. Living long enough to realize finally the full implications of mass "motopian" expansion, Wright had cause to regret the buoyancy of his casual observation in part four of *The Living City* to the effect that "America needs no help to Broadacre City; it will haphazardly build itself. Why not plan it?" But planning, of course, was the one thing that consumerism could hardly bring itself to do, and so Wright lived to witness the first haphazard encroachments of the megalopolis upon the panorama of his beloved Taliesin West.

Notes

1. Frank Lloyd Wright, *The Story of the Tower: The Tree That Escaped the Crowded Forest* (New York: Horizon Press, 1956), 12.

2. Wright, *The Story of the Tower*, 15–16.

3. Frank Lloyd Wright, *A Testament* (New York: Horizon Press, 1957), 186.

4. Wright, *A Testament*, 191.

SIR EDWIN LUTYENS ARCHITECT

To appraise the work of this great Englishman, I am incompetent. Sir Edwin so thoroughly expressed the cultural feeling of the better English of his day that a new-world reaction like mine could not be trusted to do more than voice admiration of the love, loyalty and art with which this cultured Architect, in love with Architecture, shaped his buildings.

To him the English chimney, the Gable, the Gatepost monumentalized in good brick-work and cut-stone were motifs to be used with great skill. He was able to dramatize them with a success unequalled.

Nor can I think of anyone able to so characteristically and quietly dramatize the old English feeling for dignity and comfort in an interior, however or wherever that interior might be in England. I have much admired the way in which his passion for Tradition thus graciously fitted its place in his own country.

But when his great talents were employed in India I do not feel this admiration. It seems to me the work in Delhi showed him as strange to the land as the land was strange to him.

The English Arts and Crafts owe Sir Edwin a great debt of gratitude. He insisted upon good craftsmanship at a time

"Sir Edwin Lutyens Architect," review of Lutyens's *Memorial Volumes* in *Building Magazine* (July 1951); the draft held by the Avery Library is dated to May 30, 1951.

Wake Up, Wisconsin

By FRANK LLOYD WRIGHT

HOW those who love this great State, jealous of its honor, can tolerate Wisconsin politics now is beyond a brain and heart like mine. Our public-enemy-number-one is no ISM. No, our worst enemy is the craven credulity of our citizenry. Fear is the real danger in any democracy. Our worst enemy now is this craven fear managed by conscienceless politicians.

Scare the mob! Huddle the timid voters at the polls and a politician gets what he wants by exploiting their fears. Look the credulity of this present stampede full in the face and see our public-enemy-number-one. Mobocracy, afraid, can always bid more votes than true democracy, unless aroused, can ever hope to counteract.

Frank Lloyd Wright

*   *   *

NOT so long ago Wisconsin had the reputation of a great and noble State. Government by great individuals came from the aroused democratic heart of the State. It is now coming from demagoguery at the mobocratic level. Today, by the popular electoral record, Wisconsin is a stench in the nostrils of decency everywhere. Blame is not so much to the frightened mob knowing no better. Shame goes to those knowing better, yet, to aid their own political fortunes, willing to play the ISMIC game to further exploit the multitude. Today the great name Wisconsin, well earned, stands more for damage to America by a deliberate, dishonest exaggeration of the significance, therefore the power, of communism than exists in any other State in the world.

*   *   *

THESE fighters of communism! Do they really know what communism means? Ask them. Their answers will make you laugh. Do they know what democracy means? Ask them and weep.

Fighters? Any rat will turn and fight. We are the victims of moral cowards putting up a sham fight. Well—an ISM exploited for political purposes is great Wisconsin's shame now. This political scare huddles Wisconsin's timid voters at the polls like nothing else. A principle, violate, or inviolate, will move the mobocratic mass no longer. Low-level politicians knew this well enough to prostitute the nobility of a great State.

*   *   *

On what level are her citizens now represented? But, after all, why blame anyone but ourselves for this degradation? We as citizens have only ourselves to blame for these losses politically, educationally, yes, and morally.

This huddle of timid voters at the primaries scared into voting for self-seeking rousers playing upon their timidity instead of for upright, far-sighted statesmen telling unpleasant truths.

We are now marked not by great names of noble statesmen and famed as the home of great individuals, but by inciters of a sacred people.

*   *   *

AS AN architect, therefore, I submit a simple design for a suitable and perhaps salutary memorial to the chief demagogue in the prevalent ISMIC stampede. Here it is: At all principal cross-roads of the State set up, on a solid concrete base, a large cast iron pot of simple but chaste design, say 6 feet in diameter. Pour into it a powerful charge of H2S or carbon dioxide. On the birthday of the chief demagogue of the prevalent ISM over the entire area of the State light a blaze under every pot and raise such a prodigious stink that the true character of such a "patriot" would be brought to the noses of the voters, there where they might actually realize the nature of his "patriotism" by their own nausea. This realistic celebration to continue for 24 hours or for long enough to bring to the voters realization of the character of such "patriotism."

*   *   *

WHAT great State has not been eventually ruined by the " "patriotism" of conscienceless public-servants? History has no conflict on this point. All have died of exploited FEAR.

"Wake Up, Wisconsin," published in *The Capital Times*, September 22, 1952. The front page editorial warns against the dangers of McCarthyism: "Fear is the real danger in any democracy. Our worst enemy now is this craven fear managed by conscienceless politicians."

Frank Lloyd Wright never went to se
Fair (Columbian Exposition, 1891–93)
the view of it, above, is typical of the
he formulated his principles of architec
1894. State Street in Chicago, where
looked like the drawing below

"Organic Architecture Looks at Modern Architecture," in *Architectural Record*, vol. 111, no. 5 (May 1952): 148–154.

Few realize that the principles of Wright's "organic architecture" were actually written in 1894. They were first published in an article by Wright in ARCHITECTURAL RECORD, March 1908, and are republished here (top of succeeding pages), along with his current article. His credo, dated 1894 but difficult to improve upon today, is important background for his criticism of the contemporary architectural scene.

IC ARCHITECTURE LOOKS AT MODERN ARCHITECTURE

Frank Lloyd Wright

N-ARCHITECTURE is the offspring of Organic-itecture: an offspring, already emasculate and alized, in danger of becoming a Style. Having many styles since Old Colonial washed up on d Mission reappeared on western shores, this akes over another one — this time the 58th -derived from its own exported Organic-re.

-architecture was Middle West. Out of the of Democracy" at the end of the nineteenth eginning of the twentieth century, came this e of architecture. Gradually, over a fifty-year period of ambiguous acceptance and university it planted and established fertile forms and opriate methods for the natural (machine) use glass, plastics (like concrete) and provided ole freedom in shelter for the free new life of ted States than any "style" had ever provided promised. Organic-architecture thus came of — a new freedom for a mixed people living a

new freedom under a democratic form of life. Susceptible of infinite variety, it changed the proportions of building throughout the world. The Machine was dedicated to it. Grandomania dead of it — or dying.

Organic-architecture was definitely a new sense of shelter for *humane* life. Shelter, broad and low. Roofs either flat or pitched, hipped or gabled but always comprehensive Shelter. Wide flat eaves were sometimes perforated to let trellised light through upon character-istic ranges of windows below. Ornament was non-exist-ent unless integral. Walls became screens, often glass screens, and the new open-plan spread space upon a con-crete ground-mat: the whole structure intimate and wide upon and of the ground itself. This ground-mat floor eventually covered and contained the gravity-heating system (heat rises naturally as water falls) of the spaces to be lived in: forced circulation of hot water in pipes embedded in a broken stone bed beneath the floor slabs (soon misnamed "radiant-heat"). Other new

A CONVERSATION

Frank Lloyd Wright: Come in, Hugh.

Hugh Downs: Hello, Mr. Wright.

Wright: Glad to see you.

Downs: Glad to see you.

Wright: What's that you have in your hand?

Downs: I have a book here I'm going to ask you a question about in just a moment. I thought in the brief space of a half hour which is the time we have, what we'd like to do, Mr. Wright, is get as clear a picture as possible, for our audience, of the essence of your thinking about architecture . . . about American architecture in American life.

Wright: In a half hour?

Downs: Well, as much as we are able to do in a half hour. Would you identify this picture for us?

"A Conversation with Hugh Downs," in *The Future of Architecture*, published by Horizon Press in New York, 1953. The conversation was originally broadcast on NBC on May 17, 1953.

THE NATURAL HOUSE

FRANK
LLOYD
WRIGHT

The Natural House, published by Horizon Press in New York, 1954.

125

Hardcover binding of *The Living City* with a sketch by Wright indicating the
preferred placement of his iconic red square logo; published by Horizon Press
in New York, 1958.

FRANK
LLOYD
WRIGHT
THE
LIVING CITY

The Living City with dust jacket, published by Horizon Press in New York, 1958.

St. Mark's Tower, Project,
New York City, 1929

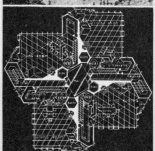

The Story of the Tower: The Tree That Escaped the Crowded Forest, published by Horizon Press in New York, 1956. The project illustrated his unbuilt proposal for St. Mark's-in-the-Bouwerie, 1927–31.

Principle is the only safe tradition.   Organic architecture —
natural architecture—is capable of infinite variety in concept and
form but faithful always to principle. It is—in fact and in deed—
itself principle. A natural architecture true to the nature of the
problem, to the nature of the site, of the materials and of those for
whom it is built—in short, of the Time and Place and Man. Building *of* these, not applied or imposed *on* them. Neither a mere facade
nor a glass poster, set up or "put over," regardless of man or the
elements in which he must live—and built regardless of the basic
principles which are the blood and the sinews of architecture
organic.

By way of illuminating this perennial — eternal — matter of
principle inherent in the solution of any problem, principle which
lives and refuses to compromise wherever compromise is death to
the integrity of the concept, here is The Tower as "idea." Not since
I first began to think around it and work on aspects of the structure
in 1891 with Lieber Meister, Louis Sullivan; but since this form
first took shape for me in the design of St. Mark's-on-the-Bouwerie:

1929

Here is a fresh development of "St. Mark's", the now realized
design of individual modern building for centralization or decen-
tralization that, as a type, fulfills modern requirements either way
and utilizes machine age resources at work upon machine age
materials in a characteristic machine age way! The straight line
and flat plane architecture suited to the technique of the machine
age is seen here in significant outline instead of monumental mass.

For sources of this text, see page 134.

129

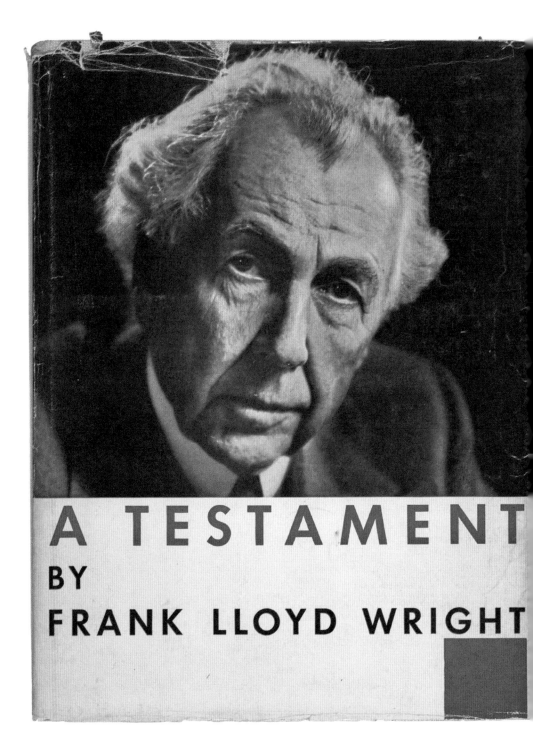

A TESTAMENT

BY

FRANK LLOYD WRIGHT

130   *A Testament*, published by Horizon Press in New York, 1957.

Wright in Retrospect

The essays in this book trace the complex evolution of Frank Lloyd Wright's intellectual trajectory with an emphasis on the culture-politics that permeated his thought and work, from his late nineteenth century start to his mid-twentieth century end. Wright grappled with the ideological foundations of his architecture in writing, and at the same time he was keenly aware of the need to discriminate between building and writing when it came to the realization of architectural form. In *An Organic Architecture: The Architecture of Democracy*, he writes: "I find it safer to try to build than to try to 'say it' because in construction sophistry falls down whereas tactful language has the disconcerting knack of outliving itself."[1] Even so, we are able to better understand Wright as a builder by revisiting his extensive literary output, through which he attempted to ground the practice of architecture more solidly in the political, technological, and social world he was surrounded by.

Throughout his long career, Wright thought up one seminal concept after another, and these paradigms continued to ricochet in his architecture throughout the first half of the twentieth century. Wright continually invented new prototypical forms in response to the changing conditions of modern society, from the modern office building demanded by the rise of the so-called "service industry" to domestic type-forms appropriate to the ceaseless expansion of suburbia. Thus Wright found himself confronted at the ideational level with three categorically modern and programmatically interrelated prototypes: first, a new middle-class house appropriate to the emerging mass society; second, a new kind of land-settlement pattern suitable for the ever-expanding megalopolis beyond the confines of the historic city; and third, the open bureaucratic landscape, a new place of work, which Walter Benjamin would characterize as a fundamental shift in the gravitational center of reality: from the home to the office.

While the first of these challenges led to his formulation of the Prairie House of 1901 as an open plan around a central fireplace, the second came to the fore with his entry for the residential land-settlement competition organized by the City Club of Chicago in 1913. This orthogonally gridded, park-like residential scheme, featuring quadripartite clusters of his Prairie House, was in fact imagined as an alternative to the Anglo-Saxon garden city paradigm first posited diagrammatically by Ebenezer Howard in 1898 and later built-out as an unconvincingly picturesque composition in Raymond Unwin's Letchworth Garden City of 1910. As for the new office building, this was first fully articulated in the eight-story Larkin Building that he designed and realized for the Martin mail-order company in Buffalo in 1904.

The Larkin Building also happened to be Wright's first introspective "public" building, the last of which was the Guggenheim Museum, realized at the end of his life. Both buildings present the public with a silent, virtually windowless façade, a quality shared with Wright's Unity Temple (1904–1906). Significantly, the honorific representation of these three institutions is categorically displaced to the layered interior extending the full height of each work. This new space of public appearance is first worked out in the Larkin Building, where, despite its secular nature, it is rendered as if it were a transcendental Unitarian house of worship, with ideological inscriptions extending from the fountains of the twin entry courts to the spandrels of the atrium's upper tiers. And at one point in its history, the Martin Company even saw fit to install a pipe organ high up beneath the glass roof of the atrium.

Like Louis Sullivan, Wright believed that the dawning American century had the potential to create a uniquely modern machine-age civilization, one that was capable of rivalling the indisputably great civilizations of the past, above all those ancient cultures of the Middle and Far East, both Islamic and pre-Islamic, and also, in the unique case of Wright, the surviving ethos of American Indian culture in the canvas-covered, timber-battened, mono-pitched forms we find in his Ocotillo Camp, Chandler, Arizona of 1929 and in Taliesin West, Scottsdale, Arizona of 1938. Here the cacti and the petroglyphic rocks of the Sonoran Desert afforded Wright with what he saw as an exotic "tabula rasa" upon which to erect his textillic interpretation of an aboriginal American world.

Wright's first projection of a modern American utopia was surely the Wolf Lake Amusement Park of 1895, commissioned by the real estate magnate E. C. Waller, for a lake on the Illinois-Indiana state line. This was inspired by Daniel Burnham and Frederick Law Olmsted's Columbian World Exhibition of 1893, as we may judge from the romantic grandeur of Wright's aerial perspective, which also anticipates Jules Guérin's sublime renderings of Daniel Burnham's Chicago Plan of 1909. Of this romantic panorama Bruce Brooks Pfeiffer has written:

> The first design that Wright proposed was a large half circle nestled into the shoreline of the lake. Within this half circle were all the concessions of the amusement park, including a bandstand, racetrack, viewing stand, casinos and covered pavilions. Two long arms protruded out onto the

lake as beaches with bathing pavilions. Bridges over water connected the central circle with its bandstand, racetrack and viewing stand to a spacious mall and concessions contained within the half circle. Tall towers carrying lights and balloons placed throughout the park added a festive element.[2]

It is characteristic of Wright's perennial *Gesamtkunstwerk* that the lower two-thirds of this aerial perspective should be taken up by the lake itself. Upon the surface of the lake the draughtsman saw fit to set a pleasure steamer, the functional lines of which were at variance with the ethos of Wright's waterfront park. The project was fatefully conceived like the Midway Gardens, Chicago of 1915, which was also realized for Waller as a total work of art.

Although there is nothing remotely Japanese about the Wolf Lake proposal, it anticipated Wright's susceptibility to the cult of "Japanism" after his first visit to Japan in 1905 — in as much as the quasi-abstract intensity of an artist like Hokusai would haunt him for the rest of his life. He had by then already experienced "traditional" Japanese architecture in the flesh, in the form of the Ho-o-den transshipped to Chicago by the Japanese government and re-erected by Japanese carpenters on a prominent site in Chicago's Columbian World Exhibition. It would seem that witnessing the pavilion being built combined with his awareness of advances in wood-working machinery during the late 1880's inspired him to argue in his 1901 address "The Art and Craft of the Machine" that the sophisticated use of wood-working machines would ultimately enable American craftsmen to produce the same highly-refined timber finish as was wrought by the hand of Japanese carpenters. This was the essential redeeming message of his address, that the machine itself will enable us to transcend the industrial furor and environmental degradation that had marked the end of the century.

Wright's vision of a new machine-age civilization assumed a particularly exotic form during his Californian episode of the early 1920s, beginning with his Hollyhock House built for the heiress Aline Barnsdall in 1920. Conceived as the prestigious home for the beneficent patron of a cultural enclave in Southern California, one that regrettably was never realized, the Hollyhock House effectively initiated Wright's experimentation with precast textile concrete blocks — leading to four concrete block houses built in short order in 1924, the first one in Pasadena and the rest in Los Angeles. Wright would finally return to his native Midwest just before the economic disaster of 1929, where he conjured up the last domestic invention of his life, namely the Malcolm Willey House. This was first designed in 1932 on two levels, with living above and bedrooms below, only to be immediately reworked as a single story house elevated on a shallow podium. This was in effect his first "Usonian" house — a term introduced by Wright to describe his vision of an idealized American style in the series of essays written for *Architectural Record* under the title, "In The Cause of Architecture." Five years later, Wright built the first automotive, "patio" house for Herbert Jacobs in Madison, Wisconsin in 1937, in which an open, L-shaped plan, a built-in ergonomic kitchen, and a bookcase occupying an entire wall of the living space may now be seen as Wright's ultimate attempt to render the American suburb as a place of civility. Surely, this is the only element of Wright's Broadacre City thesis that appears to be as essentially viable now as it was when it was first realized. Conceived as a non-airconditioned environment and somewhat inadequately insulated with its triple layered board and battened walls, it was ultimately justified by Wright on the grounds that one only needed to keep one's feet warm. This last condition he achieved through a continuous reinforced concrete ground slab with cast-in-place piped circuitry, which would be charged with hot water in winter and cold water in summer. Thus despite its inherent individualism and its dependence on the automobile, the Usonian House was nonetheless a proto-ecological, economical proposition, constructed largely out of brick and timber, materials which are now known to be those with the least embodied energy.

Such is the exoticism of Wright's vision that the last significant work of his career, namely the Guggenheim Museum realized in the year of his death, would in effect be based on an inversion of his Gordon Strong Automobile Object projected for the flat expanse of the Midwestern prairie in 1925. This design assumed the form of a ziggurat, with a car ramp spiraling up to the top from which one could enjoy an unobstructed view of the landscape in every possible direction. This form, borrowed from the Middle East, was turned inside out by Wright in order to create the Guggenheim, with visitors descending on foot down the continuous pedestrian ramp from the apex of the atrium, where it is at its widest dimension, down to its narrowest sweep at the level of the ground floor. Thus everything about the cross section of the museum justifies it being provocatively labelled "taruggiz," which is the word "ziggurat" spelled backwards. The ramp, which terminates at grade just before the outline of a fountain pool, metamorphoses Sullivan's evocation of the Sycamore "seed-germ" as the ultimate basis of a biomorphic,

democratic civilization based on the expression of individual character —
confirmation once again of an all-pervasive metaphor of organicism and
nature worship that informs to a similar degree the cosmological, and
highly political, corpus of the Wrightian endeavor.

— Kenneth Frampton
    New York, 2017

Notes

1. See page 81 for the forward to *An Organic Architecture: The Architecture of Democracy* (London: Lund Humphries, 1939).
2. Bruce Brooks Pfeiffer, *Frank Lloyd Wright: Complete Works 1885–1916*, vol. 1 (Hong Kong and Los Angeles: Taschen, 2009), 67.

Select Bibliography

Baker Brownell and Frank Lloyd Wright, *Architecture and Modern Life* (New York and London: Harper & Brothers, 1937).

William Chaitkin, "Frank Lloyd Wright in Russia," *Architectural Association Quarterly*, vol. 5, no. 2 (April-June 1973): 45–55.

Roger Cranshaw, "Frank Lloyd Wright's Progressive Utopia," *Architectural Association Quarterly*, vol. 10, no. 1 (1978): 3–9.

Henry-Russell Hitchcock, *In the Nature of Materials, 1897–1941: The Buildings of Frank Lloyd Wright* (New York: Duell, Sloan and Pearce, 1942).

Neil Levine, *The Urbanism of Frank Lloyd Wright* (Princeton, NJ: Princeton University Press, 2015).

Jonathan Lipman, *Frank Lloyd Wright and the Johnson Wax Buildings* (New York: Rizzoli, 1986).

Bruce Brooks Pfeiffer, ed., *Letters to Apprentices: Frank Lloyd Wright* (Fresno, CA: Press at California State University, 1982); and Pfeiffer, *Letters to Architects: Frank Lloyd Wright* (Fresno, CA: Press at California State University, 1984).

John Sergeant, *Frank Lloyd Wright's Usonian Houses: The Case for Organic Architecture* (New York: Whitney Library of Design, 1975).

Image Credits

Documents in the Avery Drawings and Archives are cataloged as follows:

p. 25: "The Architect and the Machine," item 2401.001, version A.

p. 26: "Architecture, Architect and Client," item 2401.004, version A.

p. 27: "The Art and the Craft of the Machine," item 2401.008, version A.

p. 28: "A Philosophy of Fine Art," item 2401.011, version A.

p. 29: "Introduction to German Monograph of 1910," item 2401.017, version B.

p. 34: "The New Imperial Hotel in Tokyo," item 2401.481, version A.

p. 35: "In The Cause of Architecture: I. The Logic of the Plan," item 2401.040, version C.

p. 46: "Poor Little American Architecture," item 2401.065, version B.

p. 47: "Style in Industry," item 2401.069, version A.

p. 48: "The Cardboard House," item 2401.070, version A.

p. 49: "To the Young Man in Architecture," item 2401.081, version B.

p. 50–57: Early design schemas for *An Autobiography*, items 3401.005, 3104.010, 3104.006, 3104.009, 3401.001.

p. 71: "The Hillside Home School of the Allied Arts," item 2401.056, version A.

p. 72: "Of Thee I Sing," item 2401.334, version J.

p. 74: "Pravda Questionnaire," item 2401.135, version B.

p. 75: "Pravda Questionnaire," item 2401.135, version F.

p. 77: "To the Memorial Craftsmen of America," item 2401.189, version A.

p. 78: "For Izvestia," item 2401.203, version A.

p. 97: "Wake Up America!," item 2401.242, version G.

p. 99: "Usonia, Usonia South And New England," item 2401.254, version D.

p. 104–105: "A Taliesin Square-Paper #3," item 2401.574, version C.

p. 106: "Defense," item 2401.574, version D.

p. 108: "Prejudice, Sir, Is A Disease," item 2401.287, version A.

p. 109: "AIA Gold Medal Acceptance Speech," item 2401.291, version A.

p. 120: "Sir Edwin Lutyens Architect," item 2401.302, version A.

p. 121: "Wake Up, Wisconsin," item 2401.309, version C.

Acknowledgments

I must first thank the Avery Architectural and Fine Arts Library, specifically Carole Ann Fabian (Director) and Janet Parks (Curator of Drawings and Archives), without which this project would not be possible. Margaret Smithglass, Shelley Hayreh, Teresa Harris, and Lena Newman have also been instrumental in helping us identify and gather materials for this book. The accessibility of Wright's Archive in Avery Library continues to spark new trajectories through his extensive oeuvre. The photographic eye of Dwight Primiano cannot be underestimated—he continues to transform our understanding of Wright's work through his remarkable grasp of the materiality of this equally remarkable collection.

I am indebted to Barry Bergdoll and Carole Ann Fabian for their generous contributions to this publication. However, my debt to Barry Bergdoll extends beyond this occasion in that his seminal essay of 1982 on the influence of Gottfried Semper on the architectural culture of the Chicago School prompted me to include Wright in my inquiry into the evolution of tectonic theory as published a decade later in 1992.

Frank Lloyd Wright has inspired a wealth of scholarly writing far too extensive to note here. However, I would like to signal my personal appreciation for Anthony Alofsin, whose work was essential in the initial formulation of these essays, and who, in effect, encouraged me to republish them today in the form of five consecutive texts.

Columbia Books on Architecture and the City
An imprint of the Graduate School of Architecture, Planning, and Preservation
Columbia University
1172 Amsterdam Ave
407 Avery Hall
New York, NY 10027

arch.columbia.edu/books

Distributed by Columbia University Press
cup.columbia.edu

Wright's Writings: Reflections on Culture and Politics 1894–1959
By Kenneth Frampton

Design: Luke Bulman—Office
Copyeditor: Walter Ancarrow

978-1-941332-35-1

This book has been produced through the Office of the Dean, Amale Andraos, and
the Office of Publications at Columbia University GSAPP.

Director of Publications: James Graham
Managing Editor: Jesse Connuck
Associate Editor: Isabelle Kirkham-Lewitt

Library of Congress Cataloging-in-Publication Data

Names: Wright, Frank Lloyd, 1867–1959, author. | Frampton, Kenneth. | Fabian,
    Carole Ann. | Bergdoll, Barry.
Title: Wright's writings : reflections on culture and politics 1894–1959 /
    Kenneth Frampton.
Description: New York, NY : Columbia Books on Architecture and the City,
    2017. | Includes bibliographical references and index.
Identifiers: LCCN 2017021704 | ISBN 9781941332351 (pbk. : alk. paper)
Subjects: LCSH: Wright, Frank Lloyd, 1867–1959—Philosophy.
Classification: LCC NA737.W7 A35 2017 | DDC 720.92—dc23
LC record available at https://lccn.loc.gov/2017021704

10 9 8 7 6 5 4 3 2 1